Good Grammar in One Hour

With a welcom...
with a no-nons...
Good Grammar ...
and user-friendl...
in decades. Des...
limited time to s......... both an update and
a crash course on all the grammar needed to speak
and write clearly, expressively and elegantly.

The **One Hour Wordpower** *series*

One Hour Wordpower

Good Grammar
in One Hour

GRAHAM KING

Mandarin
in association with
The Sunday Times

A Mandarin Paperback
GOOD GRAMMAR IN ONE HOUR

First published in Great Britain 1993
by Mandarin Paperbacks
an imprint of Reed Consumer Books Ltd
Michelin House, 81 Fulham Road, London SW3 6RB
and Auckland, Melbourne, Singapore and Toronto

Reprinted 1993

Copyright © Graham King 1993
The right of Graham King to be identified
as the Author of these works has been asserted
in accordance with the Copyright, Designs
and Patents Act 1988

A CIP catalogue record for this title
is available from the British Library
ISBN 0 7493 1520 2

Printed and bound in Great Britain
by Cox & Wyman Ltd, Reading, Berks

This book is sold subject to the condition
that it shall not, by way of trade or otherwise,
be lent, resold, hired out, or otherwise circulated
without the publisher's prior consent in any form
of binding or cover other than that in which
it is published and without a similar condition
including this condition being imposed
on the subsequent purchaser.

Contents

Acknowledgements

Consultant on Grammar and Linguistics:
Paul Coggle, Senior Lecturer in German,
University of Kent at Canterbury.

Introduction

Learning and obeying all the rules of grammar will not automatically bestow excellence on your speech and writing; but completely ignoring them will almost certainly consign you to inarticulate semi-illiteracy.

Users of the English language tend to fall into three groups. The smallest consists of those who really care about the language even to the extent of believing they are its guardians. To them a mispronounced word, a split infinitive, a double negative, are anathema.

Slightly larger, probably, is the group that neither knows nor gives a damn about correct usage; yet, paradoxically, it is the one that contributes more colour and consternation and more new words and novel expressions to the language than the others, even though, initially at any rate, its offerings may be as welcome as a coachload of shellsuit yobbos.

By far the largest group are those who retain an awareness of the language, some respect for correct spelling and pronunciation and who on occasions will consciously do, or think of doing, something about improving their mastery of English and its grammar. Members of this group probably own dictionaries.

Good Grammar in One Hour has been written with all three groups in mind. Many of the 'don't cares' would love to kick some words around if they could only find a book or course that made grammar accessible, interesting and understandable.

Even among our top group there are many people who are enviably articulate and fluent yet often find themselves at a loss over some grammatical point. For these people, as with those in the large middle group, *Good Grammar in One Hour* will provide the missing or forgotten knowledge without the need for a long and laborious re-education.

Not even the highest grammatical authorities can ever claim they know it all. H. W. Fowler, the doyen of correct usage, and Robert Burchfield, compiler of the great *Oxford English Dictionary*, have both suffered the embarrassment of making the most rudimentary mistakes. A Mensa advertisement asked: '*Can you solve this problem faster than me?*' (Grammatically punctilious, *Me* was boggled!) Even *The Times*, that paragon of grammatical certitude, trips up with comforting regularity. It recently wrote, 'According to the Adult Literacy and Basic Skills Unit, one in four 16- to 20-year-olds have reading problems and more than one third have trouble with spelling.' (*have* should read *has*). To make matters worse it appeared in an editorial on the need for the rigorous teaching of grammar.

None of us can ever assume we're on top of a pernickety language that chops trees down and then chops them up; that has parents telling their children to sit down at the meal table and to then sit up; that has marriages breaking down and then breaking up; that has court cases open and shut at the same time; and has some unfortunate with a toothache pondering over the dentist's remark that the extraction will be 'fairly painless'. Either it's going to hurt or it isn't.

This is what usage is all about, and it's what makes our language so frustrating but at the same time so fascinating. Every day it changes, perhaps imperceptibly, and we all contribute to the changes. If enough of us, a majority, insist that black means white, then, the linguists say, it *does* mean white, and the old meaning goes out of the window. This is why, today, most books on grammar avoid insisting that this usage is 'correct' and that usage is 'wrong'. *Good Grammar in One Hour* doesn't completely go along with this, believing that most readers will have bought this book for some positive straightforward guidance. However, every reader is also free to disagree with it.

Good Grammar in One Hour has been designed as a refresher course, a fast update or a kickstart, depending upon your needs and your present relationship with the language. It does not set out to teach, but to convey, step by step, a lively awareness of the workings of grammar and the possibilities of using it to improve your speaking, writing and reading.

The text has been subjected to some extensive road testing, and care has been taken to keep grammatical terms to a minimum. In the interests of simplicity the term grammar (and grammarian) is used in the widest sense, encompassing, at times, syntax, morphology, phonology, semantics and orthography. You should be so lucky.

What is Grammar?
Why Use It?

This won't take long.

A language requires two elements to fulfil virtually all the needs of communication – a vocabulary and a grammar.

The vocabulary is the language's stock of words: combinations of symbols, signs or letters that have meanings that identify things and ideas. But words by themselves can never constitute a language. Imagine somebody having all the words required to express the message in the first sentence, but no method of putting them together. An attempt might look like this:

> Grammar about what what time take long no little yes

It would be like trying to build a wall with tennis balls. What is needed is some cement or glue to stick them together. In the case of a language this glue is a mixture of rules called grammar.

Languages aren't created in a day; some evolve over hundreds, even thousands of years. The users of a language must invent all the time, and when they don't invent they borrow. English has borrowed from just about every language on earth. Not only words were purloined, but rules, too. English grammar contains rules that can be traced back to the Greeks and Romans: rules that helped the early users of our language to string their words together to create more complex and clearer messages. They enabled that meaningless jumble of words above to take shape as a recognisable sentence:

> I tell you what grammar is will need not little time not long time but some time

An improvement, but still the language required some more words and rules. The speaker wanted something more precise than *tell*, like *explain*. Also needed was a system for building phrases with their own meanings, and another system for adding inflections to basic words: *explain*, *explaining*, *explained*. With such improvements, the sentence becomes shorter but also more accurate:

> Explaining what grammar is will not take a long time.

Then users began to get really clever by inventing idioms like *not too long* to say in three words what it took nine words to say in an earlier version. They also learned to relate sentences to each other. Having asked the question in the chapter headline, why should the opening sentence repeat the same information? So we arrive at:

> What is Grammar? Why use it? This will not take long.

And, then, finally, in the quest for even greater economy, the newly invented apostrophe was brought into play, saving yet one more word:

> This won't take long.

None of this will surprise you, because if you are a native user of English you are also an intuitive user of its grammar, and probably a very skilful user, too. Nevertheless, this quick dip into the origins of grammar will provide a foundation for all that follows in this book.

The Thirteen Gremlins of Grammar

1. Correct speling is essential.
2. Don't use no double negatives.
3. Verbs has got to agree with their subjects.
4. Don't write run-on sentences they are hard to read.
5. About them sentence fragments
6. Don't use commas, that aren't necessary.
7. A preposition is not a good word to end a sentence with.
8. Remember to not ever split infinitives.
9. Writing carefully, dangling participles must be avoided.
10. Use apostrophe's correctly.
11. Make each singular pronoun agree with their antecedents.
12. Join clauses good, like a conjunction should.
13. Proofread your writing to make sure if you words out.

And, above all, avoid clichés like the plague.

You Know More About Grammar Than You Think

Although you may not know what a prepositional complement is or what it does, and may never have heard of subordinator conjunctions or modal auxiliaries, it is nevertheless very likely that you know a lot more about grammar than you think you do.

Whether your memories of what you were taught about English grammar are fresh or distantly hazy, pleasant or mordantly painful, a good deal of it has undoubtedly stuck. And on this foundation, through daily conversation, reading newspapers and watching television, you have, if you are an ordinary person, built up a handy working knowledge of grammar.

To demonstrate this to yourself, try the following test, consisting of twenty examples of right and wrong grammatical use of the language. A tip before you begin: rather than try to analyse the examples, try to 'listen' to what is being said.

(Answers and Score Sheet, pages 20–23)

1. One of these isn't a sentence. Which one is?

   A. *Any failure of the buyers to comply with any of the conditions, the damages are recoverable by the seller or the Auctioneers.*

   B. *Any failure of the buyers to comply with any of the conditions may result in damages recoverable by the seller or the Auctioneers.*

2. Here's another pair of sentences. One contains a fairly common mistake. Which is correct?

   A. *On Sunday we heard the first chaffinch sing, we have several that come into the garden for crumbs.*

   B. *On Sunday we heard the first chaffinch sing; we have several that come into the garden for crumbs.*

3. This one demands closer inspection. Which one do you think is considered correct?

   A. *A thousand visitors are not unusual on an average weekday.*

   B. *A thousand visitors is not unusual on an average weekday.*

4. You can add to your score by spotting the inconsistency in one of these sentences. Which is consistent?

   A. *The team, which is playing in Manchester next week, were badly out of form on their last performance.*

   B. *The team, which is playing in Manchester next week, was badly out of form on its last performance.*

5. If you read these sentences carefully, you will see that one doesn't make sense. Which one is clear and correct?

   A. *She remained unimpressed by both evidence and argument.*

   B. *She remained both unimpressed by evidence and argument.*

6. Because it asks you to decide between who and whom, this question is one of the toughest in the test. But try, anyway, to pick the correct usage:

   A. *The Foreign Secretary, whom we are pleased to see is now fully recovered, will speak at tonight's meeting.*

   B. *The Foreign Secretary, who we are pleased to see is now fully recovered, will speak at tonight's meeting.*

7. Here's one you should answer without even blinking. Which is correct?

   A. *The shop supplied all his shirt's and suit's and most of his ties.*

B. *The shop supplied all his shirts and suits and most of his ties.*

8. If you think about the meanings of either and neither, you should have no trouble choosing the correct sentence:

   A. *In my view either of the hotels is fine, but neither has what I would call a decent bottle of wine.*

   B. *In my view either of the hotels are fine, but neither have what I would call a decent bottle of wine.*

9. A minor error, perhaps, but it would have irked the late Graham Greene. Pick the correct statement:

   A. *Do you remember when his novel the* Third Man *came out as a movie?*

   B. *Do you remember when his novel* The Third Man *came out as a movie?*

10. One of these sentences contains two errors, so you can score 4 points by spotting them and identifying the correctly written sentence:

    A. *She would agree to go neither to the match nor to the cocktail party afterwards.*

    B. *She neither would agree to go to the match, or to the cocktail party afterwards.*

11. Back to single points for picking the correct usage of among and between.

    A. *The pudding was shared among the three of them.*

    B. *The pudding was shared between the three of them.*

12. Don't get carried away by the racy prose; there's a fundamental error in one of these sentences. Which is the sentence without the error?

    A. *Then, as he lay silently beside her, she cried: A broken, hoarse cry that sprang from a lost memory of adolescence.*

B. *Then, as he lay silently beside her, she cried: a broken, hoarse cry that sprang from a lost memory of adolescence.*

13. Try to/try and choose the correct sentence:

    A. *The teacher asked her to try to do better.*

    B. *The teacher asked her to try and do better.*

14. Question marks can be troublesome. Which sentence uses the question mark correctly?

    A. *Her mother was always asking? 'When are you going to get married.'*

    B. *Her mother was always asking, 'When are you going to get married?'*

15. There are some discordant notes in one of these sentences. Which one is consistent and harmonious?

    A. *If one is to live happily among one's neighbours, you must learn to mind your own business.*

    B. *If you are to live happily among your neighbours, you must learn to mind your own business.*

16. If you listen carefully to what is being said here, one sentence will be clear and one will confuse you. Which is the unambiguous sentence?

    A. *After the game he talked at length to the captain and the manager.*

    B. *After the game he talked at length to the captain and manager.*

17. Something weird is happening in one of these sentences. Which one avoids a rather bizarre atmospheric condition?

    A. *Tearing down the motorway at 80 mph, the fog suddenly enveloped the car, forcing me to pull over.*

B. *As I was tearing down the motorway at 80 mph, the fog suddenly enveloped the car, forcing me to pull over.*

18. Your ear should guide you here; which sentence sounds right and is right?

    A. *Penny and Tony each realised what each other was trying to do.*

    B. *Penny and Tony each realised what the other was trying to do.*

19. A somewhat strange rule is in play here, but, again, your ear should tell you which is correct:

    A. *Every man, woman and child is requested to assemble in the departure lounge.*

    B. *Every man, woman and child are requested to assemble in the departure lounge.*

20. Finally, let's find out how well you know your plurals! Which of these three sentences is correct?

    A. *One year's training is satisfactory, but three year's apprenticeship ensures greater rewards.*

    B. *One years' training is satisfactory, but three years' apprenticeship ensure greater rewards.*

    C. *One year's training is satisfactory, but three years' apprenticeship ensure greater rewards.*

If you wish to know where you stand on your knowledge and use of English grammar, you should have attempted to answer all twenty questions. If you have made a guess at some of them, don't feel too guilty: some guesses will be right and others will be wrong.

Now turn to page 21 for the answers and explanations. The correct answers to questions considered to be more difficult receive higher scores than those to easier questions.

The total score for all correct is 50. If you score 20–25 you are certainly in the 'above average' category – which means that, grammatically speaking, you are halfway there. If you score in the 25–50 range, you are among those who take considerable care over their speech and writing.

But whatever your score (even if it's 50!) you will never regret taking an hour or two to polish your native know-how of English and its workings, and to renew acquaintance with its sheer utility, its complexity, its beauty and its genius for contrariness.

Answers to the Grammar Test

Check your answers to the Grammar Test on pages 14–18 with the correct versions and explanations and enter the results on the scorecard below

Grammar Test Scorecard

Question	Score for Correct Answer	Your Score
1	3	
2	2	
3	3	
4	3	
5	2	
6	4	
7	1	
8	3	
9	2	
10	4	
11	1	
12	2	
13	2	
14	1	
15	3	
16	3	
17	2	
18	1	
19	2	
20	6	
TOTAL	50	

Answers

1. D. is a sentence. A is not because it is incomplete and makes no sense. See *Let's Look at a Sentence*.

2. A is what is called a 'run-on' sentence: the kind that someone in a state of excitement might breathlessly blurt out! It should have stopped and started again after *sing*, but as the two thoughts are closely related, the better idea is to keep them in the same sentence and separated with a longer pause – a semi-colon. So B is the sentence that is preferred.

3. B is correct. *Visitors* is plural, but *A thousand visitors* is short for 'to have a thousand visitors'. In other words the number of visitors has become a single unit, and therefore requires a singular verb, *is* and not *are*.

4. Sentence B is consistent. The problem with sentence A is that, quite correctly, it treats the team as a collective noun at the beginning (which *is* playing) but then switches to treating it as a lot of individual players (*were* badly out of form) towards the end of the sentence. See *Collective Nouns*, page 49.

5. A is quite clear and correct. If you study B closely enough you will see that it makes no sense. The only way that *both* would work in that position would be in a sentence like: *She remained both unimpressed and amused by the evidence and the argument.*

6. B is correct. In this case, apply the *he = who/him = whom* rule. As the Foreign Secretary (*he*, the subject) is fully recovered, and will speak (the object), *who* is called for. There's further discussion on the *who/whom* conundrum under *Twenty Sore Points*.

7. B is correct. The plurals of *shirt* and *suit* and *tie* are *shirts*, *suits* and *ties*. No apostrophes are needed.

8. *Either* and *neither* require singular verbs, so Sentence A, using *is* and *has* rather than *are* and *have*, is correct.

9. B is correct. The full title of Graham Greene's novel and subsequent film is *The Third Man*, not the *Third Man*.

10. A is correct on both counts. B contains what is known as a misplaced correlative (*neither would agree*), and also breaks the accepted *either/or*, *neither/nor* rule.

11. You share *between* two, or *among* three, so A is correct.

12. You capitalise at the beginning of a sentence, but not after a colon, so version B is correct.

13. Both are acceptable. The form *try to* is considered to be grammatically correct but the idiomatic *try and* is now very widely used.

14. B is correct; the question mark always follows the question.

15. B is correct. The problem with A is that the pronouns lack concord: it begins with the personal pronoun *one* but then moves on to *you* and *your*. A correct sentence using *one* would read, '*If one is to live happily among one's neighbours, one must learn to mind one's business*'. The neighbours, on the other hand, might take a dim view of anyone talking like that.

16. A is unambiguous because it makes clear that he talked to the captain *and* the manager – two people. B is unclear, because he could have talked to the captain/manager – one person.

17. The 'something weird' in one of the sentences is

the 80 mph fog tearing down the motorway!
Version B is correct. See *Danglers and Manglers*,
page 81.

18. Grammatically, A has *each other* as the subject of
the verb *realised*, which is plainly wrong and also
sounds wrong. B is right, and also sounds right.

19. A is correct, because *every* refers to each individual.
So regardless of how many men, women and
children there are, a singular verb is called for.

20. C is the sentence correct on all points. *One year's
training* requires a possessive apostrophe. So does
three years' apprenticeship, but because we now have
the plural of *year* = *years*, the apostrophe comes
after the -*s*. And because *three years' apprenticeship*
is plural, *ensure* (and not *ensures*) is needed. Getting
all this right is certainly worth a score of six!

Let's Look at Sentences

Every time we speak we use sentences. They are the easiest of all grammatical units to recognise, so it seems sensible to begin with them.

Easy to recognise, yes; but hard to define. In his *Dictionary of Modern English Usage*, H. W. Fowler gives ten definitions by various grammarians, including:

- A group of words which makes sense
- A word or set of words followed by a pause and revealing an intelligible purpose
- A combination of words that contains at least one subject and one predicate
- A combination of words which is complete as expressing a thought

None of these, however, exactly fills the bill, although it is difficult not to agree with the *Oxford English Dictionary's* definition: 'Such portion of a composition or utterance as extends from one full stop to another.'

More important is what sentences are for:

- To make statements
- To ask questions
- To request action
- To express emotion

From a practical standpoint, a sentence should express a single idea, or thoughts related to that idea. A popular rule of thumb is that a sentence should be complete in thought and complete in construction. And again, from a practical point of view, you will soon find that certain rules must be observed if your sentences are to be clear, unambiguous, logical and interesting to the listener or reader. That said, you still have plenty of scope to fashion sentences of almost any size and shape.

Here is a sentence: the opening sentence to Daniel Defoe's *The Life and strange surprising Adventures of Robinson Crusoe*.

> 'I was born in the year 1632, in the city of York,
> of a good family, though not of that country, my
> father being a foreigner of Bremen, who settled
> first at Hull: he got a good estate by merchandise,
> and leaving off his trade, lived afterward at York,
> from whence he had married my mother, whose
> relations were named Robinson, a very good family
> in that country, and from whom I was called
> Robinson Kreutznoer; but, by the usual corruption
> of words in England, we are now called, nay, we
> call ourselves, and write our name Crusoe, and so
> my companions always called me.'

Very few novelists today would have the nerve or the
skill to begin a novel with a long sentence like that; for
apart from its length it is also a skilfully wrought
passage: clear, unambiguous, supple, flowing and
ultimately riveting. If it were written today it would
most likely appear as a paragraph of several sentences:

> 'I was born in York in 1632, of a good family. My
> father came from Bremen and first settled at Hull,
> acquired his estate by trading merchandise, and
> then moved to York. There he met and married
> my mother, from a well established family in that
> county named Robinson. I was therefore named
> Robinson Kreutznoer, but in time my own name
> and that of our family was modified to Crusoe.
> That's what we are now called, that's how we write
> our name, and that's what my friends have always
> called me.'

Defoe's original is a fairly long sentence by any
standards. Now try this sentence for size:

> 'But —— !'

This one appears to defy everything we think we know
about sentences, but it is a valid sentence just the same,
as you will see when it is placed in its correct context:

> 'Jane turned abruptly from the window and faced

him with blazing eyes. "Well, you've finally done it! You realise we're all but ruined, don't you? Don't you!"

"But —— !" Harry was squirming. Speechless. He stepped back in an attempt to evade the next onslaught.

It never came. Instead, weeping uncontrollably, Jane collapsed on to the settee.'

You can see that 'But —— !', short though it is, quite adequately expresses a response and an action in the context of the second paragraph (a paragraph is a string of linked sentences with a common theme). Despite its seeming incompleteness, it is nevertheless a complete sentence in thought and construction, although some grammarians might label it a sentence fragment. Here are some more:

Her expression conveyed everything. Disaster. Ruin. Utter ruin.

Three of the four sentences above are sentence fragments. They're perfectly legitimate, but use them for emphasis only, and with care.

Another kind of sentence, and one to avoid, is seen rather too often. Typically, it is rambling and unclear, usually the result of having too many ideas and unrelated ideas jammed into it, like this one:

He said that the agreement would galvanise a new sense of opportunity and partnership between the countries and enable them to articulate the targets with regard to inflation which was always of concern to every family in the land.

Would you really bother to try to unravel that sentence? No, life is too short, and the sentence is destined to remain unread, its author's voice unheard. That's the price you pay for writing bad sentences. To demonstrate how the inclusion of irrelevant matter can cloud the intent and meaning of a sentence, consider this:

> Jonathan Yeats, whose family moved to the US from Ireland in the late 1940s, and who later married a Mormon girl from Wisconsin, wrote the novel in less than three months.

We have to ask, what has the novelist's family to do with his writing a book in record time? Did the Mormon girl help him? If not, why mention her? By the time we've reached the important part of the sentence – the fact that he wrote the book in three months – our attention has been ambushed by two extraneous thoughts.

American presidents are notorious for irrelevant rambling. The tradition began, apparently, with President Harding, of whom, when he died in 1923, a wit observed, 'The only man, woman or child who wrote a simple declarative sentence with seven grammatical errors is dead.' For example:

> 'I have had the good intention to write you a letter ever since you left, but the pressure of things has prevented, speeches to prepare and deliver, and seeing people, make a very exacting penalty of trying to be in politics.'

But we must not grieve over Harding when we have President Bush gamely carrying the national flag of Gobbledegook:

> 'I mean a child that doesn't have a parent to read to that child or that doesn't see that when the child is hurting to have a parent and help out or neither parent there enough to pick the kid up and dust him off and send him back into the game at school or whatever, that kid has a disadvantage.'

Well, enough of warnings. The point to remember is that although a sentence may be as long as a piece of string, long sentences may land you in trouble. A good sentence will be no longer than necessary, but this doesn't mean that you should chop all your sentences to a few words. That would be boring. To keep the reader alert and interested you need variety. If you examine this paragraph, for example, you will find a sentence sequence that goes *short/long/long/short/medium/long/short*. That's aiming in the right direction.

When a 'Sentence' isn't a Sentence

Here are some exceptions to all the sentences you've read so far:

> Are unable to fill any order within 21 days
> Date for the closing of
> Thinking it a good opportunity

Clearly, there's something wrong here. What is wrong is that these examples do not make sense because they are incomplete. They are incomplete because they are ungrammatical and do not adequately express a thought or carry any recognisable information. It has nothing to do with length, either; the following examples are extremely short but are grammatical and convey the intended information in such a way as to be unambiguous:

> *'Waiter!' THIS WAY   Stop!   Amount Due*

Types of Sentences

Single-word expressions like 'Hey!', signs, catchphrases, greetings and so on, are called irregular, fragmentary or minor sentences. Sentences which appear to have been constructed to express one or more thoughts are called regular or major sentences and these are our work horses for talking and writing. There is also a third type, called a compound sentence, that expresses two or more thoughts or which, grammatically, has two or more clauses. Let us take two simple, regular sentences:

> The money was spent on urban regeneration. The money provided hundreds of people with excellent houses.

Most of us, seeing these two sentences, would find it difficult to resist the urge to combine them:

> The money was spent on urban regeneration and provided hundreds of people with excellent houses.

That is a complex or compound sentence, and you will see that it links the two connected thoughts in an economical way. Indeed, a third thought could safely be added:

> The money was spent on urban regeneration and provided hundreds of people with excellent houses; but it did not take funds away from existing housing schemes.

Beyond this, you have to be careful, or risk confusing the reader. By the way, did you notice the two words that link the three sentences into one? They are *and* and *but*, and they are commonly used for building compound sentences.

Types of Regular or Major Sentences

Earlier, we defined four uses for sentences. Each of these uses calls for a type of sentence, and it's worth knowing what they are:

- A DECLARATIVE sentence makes a statement:

  A rose-bush grew in the garden.

- An INTERROGATIVE sentence asks a question:

Is that a rose-bush in the garden?

- An IMPERATIVE sentence requests or commands:

  James, dig that rose-bush out of the garden.

- An EXCLAMATIVE sentence expresses emotion:

  I wouldn't dream of touching the rose-bush!

It's also worth knowing about some other kinds of sentences:

- *I like eating at restaurants* is a positive sentence.
- *I don't like eating at restaurants* is a negative sentence.

The difference may seem obvious, but it's worth noting because a diet of too much negativism in your speech and writing can have an overall negative or depressing effect. Sometimes it is better to express a negative thought in a positive way:

She is not beautiful.

This is negative and also vague: she could be statuesque or handsome. A more positive and precise description might be:

She is rather homely.

Lastly, all sentences are either active or passive, and it is up to us to choose which 'voice' to use. Here are some examples:

ACTIVE   *The favourite won the 3.30 hurdle event.*
Her boyfriend bought the ring.
Very few can understand his poems.

PASSIVE   *The 3.30 hurdle event was won by the favourite.*
The ring was bought by her boyfriend.
His poems can be understood by very few.

It's easy to see why one sort of sentence is called active, and the other passive; active sentences are direct and seem more interesting and exciting, while passive sentences tend to be detached and impersonal. Generally, we use the active voice almost exclusively in our everyday speech and writing.

Trimming Away 'Sentence Fat'

Nobody these days wants to write more words than necessary, or to be forced to read fifty words when the information could have been conveyed in half that number. We have already seen that by combining simple sentences into compound sentences we can economise on words and even enhance clarity; but there is another grammatical convention that allows us to sensibly trim away words we don't need. It is called ellipsis, and it works like this:

WITHOUT ELLIPSIS   When the children were called to the dinner table they came to the dinner table immediately.

                                 Mr Green had more coins in his collection than Thomas had coins in his collection.

WITH ELLIPSIS   When the children were called to the dinner table they came immediately.

                                 Mr Green had more coins in his collection than Thomas had in his.

The reason we can get away with this trimming is that, if the listener or reader is paying attention, he or she will automatically supply the missing words from the context of what is being said. There is no loss of clarity, either; on the contrary, repetitive words can lead to boredom.

Sometimes our economising extends to dropping what were once considered essential words:

He was kicked out the door.
She got off the bus.

If we heard these sentences spoken in an informal context, we would hardly take exception; and, nowadays, even the strictly grammatical versions look odd to our eyes:

He was kicked out *of* the door.
She got off *of* the bus.

Another common, but quite acceptable, omission, is the word *that*:

The hat (that) she bought is a disaster.
They knew (that) they would never reach the airport in time.

Such sentences are considered informal, although their meanings are perfectly clear. If a hostess greets a guest with, '*I am delighted that you could come*', isn't she being a trifle formal? More likely, the greeting would be, '*I'm delighted you could come*'; and that is becoming the accepted usage. (The other extreme is the multiple *that*: '*He claimed that that that in the sentence was superfluous.*') If you are intent on dropping *that*, be careful (that) it doesn't lead to ambiguity.

Harmony in the Sentence

Perhaps the most important principle in the construction of sentences is what is called *concord* – which means that all the units in the sentence must agree and harmonise with each other. We can spot most inharmonious constructions, because they usually jar:

February is usually a succession of *rain, hail and snowing*.

That sentence mixes two nouns and a participle, and it

screams out at you, doesn't it? An harmonious construction would be to group three nouns:

> February is usually a sucession of *rain, hail and snow*.

Alternatively, we could use a trio of participles:

> In February, it is usually either *raining, hailing or snowing*.

Another form of discord is the shift from active to passive voice:

> My father painted those pictures, which were left to me.

That sentence mixes active and passive voice; the following sentence is consistently active, and more direct:

> My father painted those pictures and left them to me.

Other sources of discord include shifting from personal to impersonal pronouns (or vice versa): 'If one is to keep out of trouble, you should mind your p's and q's'; shifting mid-sentence from negative to positive (or vice versa); and mixing tenses. But the most common form of discord is the sentence which fails to recognise that a singular noun takes a singular verb and a plural noun takes a plural verb. The following sentences ignore this:

> *We was* furious with the umpire's decision.
> The four *houses was* sold at auction.

They should, of course, read:

> We *were* furious about the umpire's decision.
> The four houses *were* sold at auction.

But look what happens when we 'collectivise' the subjects:

The *team was* furious about the umpire's decision.
A *number* of houses *was* sold at auction.

Because we've gathered the players together into a
team, and combined the four houses into a single group
(a number), we're back to using singular verbs. This
singular/plural business is one of the trickiest areas in
the whole of grammar, and we'll have some fun with it
in the chapter on nouns.

Starting a Sentence with 'And' and 'But'

One of the more persistent grammatical superstitions is
that you can't begin a sentence with *And*. This is
curious, because many of the best writers in the English
language – Shakespeare, Blake, Tennyson, Kipling, to
name just four – have kicked sentences off with *And*,
and so has the Bible: read the opening chapter.
  The same applies to *But*:

> There is no rule to say that you can't begin a
> sentence or a paragraph with the conjunction *but*.
> When you want to express a doubt or outright
> disagreement to a statement, starting with *But* can
> emphasise and dramatise your point. *But* don't let
> it become a habit!

The *Daily Express* some years ago carried a memorable
sentence in its sporting pages that not only began with
but, but ended with *but*; and the following sentence
began with *and*:

> 'Northumberland and Humberside will each hold
> the trophy for six months after fighting out an
> exciting 1–1 draw. But if the result was indecisive,
> then the Soccer was anything but. And when all
> the medals have been engraved . . .'

The Building Blocks of Sentences: Parts of Speech

In Victorian times, when life was simpler, so, apparently, was grammar. Here is a little verse widely used to teach young children in the latter part of the nineteenth century:

> Three little words we often see,
> *Determiners* like a, an, and the.
>
> A *Noun's* the name of anything,
> A school or garden, hoop or string.
>
> An *Adjective* tells the kind of noun,
> Like great, small, pretty, white, or brown.
>
> Instead of nouns the *Pronouns* stand
> John's head, his face, my arm, your hand.
>
> *Verbs* tell of something being done,
> To read, write, count, sing, jump, or run.
>
> How things are done, the *Adverbs* tell,
> Like slowly, quickly, ill, or well.
>
> A *Preposition* stands before
> A noun, as in a room or through a door.
>
> *Conjunctions* join the nouns together,
> Like boy or girl, wind and weather.
>
> The *Interjection* shows surprise,
> Like Oh, how charming! Ah, how wise!
>
> The whole are called nine parts of speech,
> Which reading, writing, speaking teach.

This rhyme, incidentally, contains a fairly obvious grammatical error: *whole*, in the final couplet, is a 'quantity word' requiring a singular *is*, not *are*. But modernday grammarians would find far more fault with the verses than such a mere slip. 'Too simplistic', they

35

would say, and they would be right. For example, many words defy a single classification. *Play* and *première*, for example, can be nouns and adverbs:

> They looked forward to the *première* of the *play*. (nouns)
> When the play *premièred* the critics would come out to *play*. (verbs)

Modern grammar isn't so bolted down as it was, because it has to recognise changes – in the usage of words, the coining of new words, and the migration of a word from one class to another:

> The doctor noticed the *knee jerk*. (noun/verb)
> His speech produced the expected *knee-jerk* reaction. (noun used as an adjective)
> The President's campaign strategy will rely on the art of the *knee-jerk*. (noun)

This is why we now have two broad word classes: open classes (which freely admit new words) and closed classes (which rarely do). For example:

OPEN CLASSES

Nouns	*software, gazumper, Fergie, tummytuck*
Adjectives	*neural, digital, cellular, quaffable investigative, hands-on*
Verbs	*outed, overdosed, stargaze*
Adverbs	*breezily, grandly, chaotically*
Interjections	*phew, aahhh, damn, ouch*

CLOSED CLASSES

Determiners	*the, which, my, that, your, these*
Pronouns	*I, me, we, hers, someone, whom*
Conjunctions	*and, or, but, when, since, as*
Prepositions	*at, with, in, by, to, from*
Auxiliaries	*be, may, can, will, were, must*

You can see from the examples above that the closed

classes of words are more or less static; it is difficult to invent additional determiners or substitutes for *the*, *my* and *your*. The open classes, however, are expanding all the time.

At this point a pause may be useful, because we are now using grammatical terms which may mean little or nothing to you; for many of us our grasp of such terms is at best incomplete or confused, and at worst, a hazy memory. But to make sense of grammar it is difficult to avoid familiarity with at least a few basic terms. These will, however, be kept to a workable minimum.

Let us return to the components that we use as building blocks for the way we speak and write, with a simple analysis of sentences that might look like this:

An	**acting**	**spokesperson**	**for**	**the**	**Navy**
|	|	|	|	|	|
determiner	*adjective*	*noun*	*preposition*	*determiner*	*proper noun*

has	**predictably**	**outlined**	**the**	**various**	**options.**
|	|	|	|	|	|
auxiliary verb	*adverb*	*verb*	*determiner*	*adjective*	*noun*

Nouns

A noun is a name – of a place, an object, a person, an animal, a concept, of anything:

- PLACES   street, home, Germany, Paris, heaven
- OBJECTS   plate, chair, tree, chamber pot
- PERSONS   Einstein, Michael Jackson, Caroline
- ANIMALS   pony, pig, wolfhound, chimp
- CONCEPTS   option, bad temper, ability, direction

We also recognise types of nouns. All nouns are either proper nouns, or names which are quite specific,

> *Marilyn Monroe, Saturday, The Rake's Progress, Mercedes, Brooklyn Bridge, Easter*

or common nouns, which are broadly descriptive:

> *tea, coffee, hair, darkness, opinions, anger, ideas*

You'll notice that the proper nouns begin with capital letters (not invariably, however) and that the common nouns do not.

Common nouns are further subdivided into concrete, abstract, count and non-count nouns, and these are all discussed in **Naming Things – Nouns** on page 45.

Verbs

Verbs are the engines that drive sentences and make them work. Imagine trying to get through a day without these work-horses:

> *eat, drink, sleeps, dream, woke, walked, go, come, talked, do, keep*

You can see, even from these few examples, that verbs take various forms, some ending in *-s*, *-ed*, and so on, and in fact most verbs have four or more forms. For example:

> *eat, eats, eaten, ate*

If you look up the words *eats*, *eating*, *eaten* or *ate* in a dictionary, in most cases you will be referred to the base verb *eat*, where the entry will include the entire *eat* family (plus derivatives like *eatable* and *eating-house*).

Apart from their multiplicity of forms, verbs are notoriously variable: they can be regular (where they follow certain rules) and irregular (where they don't);

they can be main verbs or auxiliary verbs, transitive and intransitive, finite and infinite. But don't let these grammatical gremlins frighten you; they will be exposed for what they are in **The Business of Verbs** on page 55.

Adjectives

Life without adjectives would be very difficult and extremely dull, because adjectives describe and qualify things:

> *hot, freezing, beautiful, hairy, user-friendly, brainless, distasteful, pathogenic, pliable*

Some adjectives give themselves away by their endings: *-ing*, *-y*, *-less*, *-ful*, *-ic*, and so on. They can also end with *-ly*, and can thus be confused with adverbs, which typically end with the same suffix.

Simply put, adjectives add something to nouns by qualifying,

> It was a *dreary* match.
> We made a *late* start.

or by reinforcing a noun's descriptive power:

> It was an *obvious* mistake.
> She possessed *hypnotic* charm.

You will see that all the adjectives here come before the noun, but that need not always be the case:

> Her charm was *hypnotic*.

There is a fuller discussion of adjectives and how to use them on page 64.

Adverbs

Adverbs are close relations to adjectives, as you can see:

ADJECTIVES	ADVERBS
essential	essentially
hypnotic	hypnotically
interesting	interestingly
dark	darkly

Notice that the giveaway element in adverbs is the *-ly* ending.

The difference between adjectives and adverbs is that adjectives invariably modify nouns, while adverbs modify a range of words: verbs, adjectives and even other adverbs:

MODIFYING A VERB	He *trudged wearily* along the road.
MODIFYING AN ADJECTIVE	She's an *exceedingly lucky* girl.
MODIFYING ANOTHER ADVERB	The engine turned over *relatively smoothly*.

Adverbs are often required where adjectives are used, and vice versa. A guide to their usage will be found on page 69.

Interjections

Interjections or exclamations are self-explanatory:

Wow! Hey! Shhhh! Blimey! Oh! What?

Although these examples, expressing surprise, excitement or some other emotion, are followed by exclamation marks, these are not always necessary:

Okay, let's get on with it.
Ah-ha, that's better.

Determiners

Determiners precede nouns, and the best known and most common of them are those known as articles: *a*, *an* and *the*:

> *a* party, *an* object, *the* concert

Determiners exist, however, in some variety, and help us to indicate quantity (*some* wine); ask questions (*whose* wine?); denote possession (*my* wine); and even emotion (*what* wine!).

Pronouns

Pronouns are great stand-ins for nouns and noun phrases, and are especially useful for avoiding repetition:

WITHOUT A PRONOUN	He saw James in the bar, and went over to meet James. Was I aware that Marcia is married? Yes, I was aware that Marcia is married.
WITH A PRONOUN	He saw James in the bar, and went over to meet *him*. Was I aware that *she* is married? Yes, I was aware of *it*.

You can readily see that pronouns are indispensable, and, with determiners, form a major part of our speech.

We divide pronouns (or them) into personal pronouns (*I*, *me*, *you*, *she*, *it*); reflexive pronouns (*myself*, *themselves*); possessive pronouns (*mine*, *ours*, *his*, *theirs*); demonstrative pronouns (*this*, *these*, *those*); interrogative pronouns (*who? what? which?*); relative pronouns (*who, whom, which, that*); and reciprocal pronouns (*one another, each other*).

You may experience a prickly sensation reading this, and not without good reason, for pronouns probably create more grammatical havoc than any other class of word. See the more detailed section on pronouns on page 51, and also in **Twenty Sore Points** on page 96.

Conjunctions

Think of conjunctions as link-words that join two parts of a sentence or two nouns:

> She asked him if he intended going out *and* he told her to mind her own business.
> She told him he could stay *if* he promised to be more polite.

There are two types of conjunctions – coordinating and subordinating – which are described on page 76.

Prepositions

While conjunctions link in a fairly straightforward way, prepositions link by relating verbs to nouns, pronouns and noun phrases:

> He flew to New York *in* a 747.
> She sidled *through* the open doorway.

We use prepositions constantly (try getting through a day without using *as, by, in, on, to* and *up,* to name just a few!) and misuse them occasionally. The vexing question of whether or not you can end a sentence with a preposition is answered on page 79.

Phrases and Clauses

We have now surveyed the different kinds of words we use to construct sentences. However we should also familiarise ourselves with two units or groups of words that are usually found in sentences: phrases and clauses.

PHRASES used to be defined as a number of words working together as a unit, but today's definition includes single words. The logic of this is demonstrated when we shrink a conventional phrase:

I love *that dry white wine from California*.
I love *that white wine*.
I love *wine*.

The key word *wine* is called the headword, and because it is a noun, all three phrases are called noun phrases.

There are five types of phrases, each named after the headword:

NOUN PHRASE	their first *home* (headword *home* is a noun)
VERB PHRASE	had been *burgled* (*burgled* is a verb)
ADVERB PHRASE	very *quickly* (*quickly* is an adverb)
ADJECTIVE PHRASE	too *difficult* to do (*difficult* is an adjective)
PREPOSITIONAL PHRASE	*on* the jumbo jet (*on* is the introducing preposition, *the jumbo jet* is a noun phrase)

The popular definition of a CLAUSE is a word unit larger than a phrase but smaller than a sentence. It is also more complete than a phrase. A simple sentence contains or consists of a single clause; a multiple sentence contains two or more clauses.

Because clauses can contain several elements, including verbs, conjunctions, nouns, pronouns and adverbs, the difference between clauses and sentences can be mystifying. But clauses are not constructed with the intention of being complete in themselves, but rather as a key part, or one of several parts, of a sentence. That is why clauses are described as main clauses and subordinate clauses:

MAIN CLAUSE	SUBORDINATE CLAUSE
I'll go	*to buy the tickets*
You'll never know	*what it's like*

The whole point of clauses is that they can be strung together, but always ruled by main clauses and with as many subordinate clauses as required. Fortunately, with practice, most of us seem to acquire the skills to do this intuitively. In fact, most of us could write the following sentence, or one very much like it, without ever consciously thinking of clause construction:

The Building Societies Association was almost alone in expressing relief because it meant the scrapping of the second-phase interest rise, of 3 per cent, which was announced earlier yesterday.

Here is the above sentence (from a report in a newspaper) dissected to expose its clauses:

MAIN CLAUSE	*The Building Societies Association was almost alone in expressing relief*
SUBORDINATE CLAUSE	*because it meant the scrapping of the second-phase interest rate rise (of 3 per cent,)*
	(which was)
SUBORDINATE CLAUSE WITHIN THE SUBORDINATE CLAUSE	*announced earlier yesterday.*

44

Naming Things – Nouns

Nouns make up by far the biggest family of words in the English language. This is because nouns name things; everything, everyone, almost every place in the world has a name. The common and scientific names of all the creatures in the natural world – from elephants to insects, molluscs to mites – add another few millions to the pile. There are about two billion people living in the world and all of them have one or more names. Not all human names are unique, of course; Korea is dominated by just four surnames, and in China, combinations of surnames and given names are often shared by several hundred thousand individuals, but it still adds up to a mind-boggling total. The names or titles of every book written, every song composed, every movie made and every brand of soap powder advertised, help expand this massive lexicon by tens of thousands of new names every day of our lives.

So while our everyday working vocabulary of verbs, adjectives, adverbs and so on remains more or less static throughout our lives, new nouns continue to pour into our memory, so that a person with a working vocabulary of several thousand words might have memory access to a hundred thousand proper and common nouns.

All names are nouns, but not all nouns are names. To make the distinction we use the terms proper noun and common noun:

PROPER NOUN	COMMON NOUN
Bentley	*car*
Boeing 747	*aeroplane*
Hoover	*vacuum cleaner*
Britain	*country*
Agaricus campestris	*mushroom*
Madonna	*singer*

That is a very basic separation. But while it is easy to identify proper nouns (by their capital letters, for a start), how do we know when a word is a common noun and not an adjective or a preposition, for example?

One way to find out is to precede the word by a determiner such as *the*, *an*, *a*, or *some*:

NOUNS	NON-NOUNS
a *racehorse*	a *racing*
the *park*	the *parked*
an *assembly*	an *assemble*
some *cash*	some *cashable*

Other tests include a noun's ability to take on singular and plural form; to be replaced by pronouns (*he*, *she*, *it*, etc); and also to accept add-ons to form new nouns:

book / booking / booklet / bookman / bookmark

Nouns can also be concrete nouns, or names of things we can see and touch, like *earth*, *sky*, *vapour*, *girl* and, yes, even *concrete*; and abstract nouns, which describe concepts, ideas and qualities, like *team*, *instinct*, *strength*, *coincidence*.

Both common and proper nouns have gender, too, which we learn at a very early age:

	MASCULINE	FEMININE	NEUTER
Common nouns	*boy, bull, cock, stallion, man*	*woman, cow, hen, mare, girl*	*letter, box, gelding*
Proper nouns	*Frank Sinatra, Peeping Tom*	*Joan of Arc, Cleopatra*	*Xerox, Aida Cold War*

Another class of noun familiar to everyone is the compound noun – again demonstrating a noun's potential to grow:

gin and tonic, scotch on the rocks, ne'er-do well, Eggs McMuffin, mother-in-law, attorney general

Such nouns throw up one of the more fascinating qualities of nouns – their capacity to be countable or uncountable, and (with some exceptions) singular and plural.

Countable and Uncountable Nouns

A countable noun is usually preceded by a determiner like *a*, *an* or *the*, and can be counted, and can also have either singular or plural form:

a *hamburger*	five *hamburgers*	several *hamburgers*
an *egg*	a dozen *eggs*	a nest of *eggs*
the *mountain*	the two *mountains*	the range of *mountains*

Uncountable nouns, as the name suggests, cannot be counted, nor do they have a plural form:

music, poetry, cement, light, luck, greed

But be careful here, because nouns, including uncountable nouns, are slippery; with a deft flick of the wrist they can become:

COUNTABLE NOUNS	The ship was lit by many bright *lights*.
ADJECTIVES	Both women had *light* complexions.
VERBS	Max did his best to *light* the fire.

Singular and Plural Nouns

Of all the chameleon qualities of the countable noun, its capacity to exist in singular and plural form is perhaps the most interesting and certainly – for most of us – the most perplexing.

Singulars and plurals have for a long time provided

gamesters and wordsmiths with a favourite playground
for puzzles like these:

- Name words ending in -s which are spelt the
  same in singular and plural forms
  (Answer: *shambles*, *congeries*)
- Name a plural of a noun in which none of the
  letters are common with the singular
  (Answer: *cow* = *kine*)
- Name any plural words with no singular
  (Examples: *scissors*, *knickers*, *marginalia*)

In other words, the singular/plural phenomenon is
littered with inconsistencies. For example, most nouns
change from singular to plural by the simple addition
of an -s:

shop, shops   *boat, boats*   *gate, gates*

This is by far the largest group. Notice, by the way,
that there are no apostrophes before the -s. Then there
is another group that adds an -es to become plural:

circus, circuses   *bush, bushes*   *bus, buses*

Fair enough. But now we come to other – fortunately
smaller – groups, that pluralise in quaint and random
ways:

mouse, mice	*loaf, loaves*	*tooth, teeth*
foot, feet	*hoof, hooves*	*child, children*
ox, oxen	*medium, media*	*index, indices*
crisis, crises	*larva, larvae*	*stimulus, stimuli*

And, finally, there are nouns like *sheep* which are both
singular and plural.

We might now return to our compound nouns, which
are prone to present unusual difficulties. For example:

Is it two *gins and tonic*, please, or two *gin and
tonics*?
Is it *poet laureates* or *poets laureate*?
Is it *mother-in-laws* or *mothers-in-law*?

Is it *Egg McMuffins* or *Eggs McMuffin*?
Is it *scotches on the rocks*, or *scotch on the rocks's*?

These are conundrums that have tortured people for
ages. There is, however, a view, which sounds
reasonable, that hyphenated compounds should be
pluralised by adding an *-s* at the end (with, strangely,
the exception of *mothers-in-law*); and that unhyphenated
compounds should have the *-s* added to the central, or
most important noun. If we follow this advice, we get:

> *gins and tonic*, *poets laureate*, *Egg McMuffins* (for it
> is the McMuffin bit that creates the difference),
> and *scotches on the rocks*.

So what about *spoon full* and *mouth full*, and *spoonful*
and *mouthful*? The plurals of the first pair are *spoons
full* and *mouths full*; the point about the second pair is
fullness, so -ful is the central part of the compound
and should have the *-s* added to it: *spoonfuls* and
mouthfuls. But remember that these recommendations
are not bound by strict rules; far from it. Many
respected grammarians will opt for *spoonsful* and
mother-in-laws, and will expect to be served like anyone
else when they ask the barman for two *gin and tonics*.

Collective Nouns

There are a few other categories of nouns – nouns of a
kind, for example, like *species*, *brand*, *type* – but of
these the most useful is the collective noun. It is also a
grammatical favourite.

Collective nouns are handy because they unify things,
ideas or people into groups:

> *audience*, the *Government*, *council*, *team*, *jury*

The effect of a collective noun is to create a singular
entity, which, although many creatures (bees in *swarm*)

49

or people (members of a *jury*) are involved, should now be treated as a singular noun.

> The *army* is outside the city gates.
> Will this *class* please behave *itself*!
> The *committee* is still deliberating.

Sometimes, however, a collective noun is more subtle, and can lead to confusion:

> A vast *number* of crimes *is* never reported at all.
> The *majority* is in favour of the wage rise.

Such nouns sometimes lead to grammatically correct but odd-sounding emissions like *none of us is going to work today*, and *a lot of things is wrong with the world today*, and this in turn has led to considerable relaxation of the old rule of always following a group or collective noun with a singular verb. While not going all the way with 'if it sounds okay it *is* okay', group or collective nouns like *team*, *government* and *committee* may now be treated as singular or plural. But, once begun, don't change in midstream:

NOT	The Tilner Committee *has* a week in which to announce *their* findings.
BUT	The Tilner Committee *have* a week in which to announce *their* findings.
OR	The Tilner Committee *has* a week in which to announce *its* findings.

Collective nouns are not all doom and gloom. Knowing the correct collectives for groups of certain birds, animals and humans can score a lot of points at Wine and Wisdom nights. Try these:

a *murder* of crows	a *convocation* of eagles
an *exaltation* of larks	a *chattering* of starlings
a *pod* of whiting	a *dray* of squirrels
a *knot* of toads	a *business* of ferrets

and these, more recent, whimsical contributions:

a *rash* of dermatologists	a *piddle* of puppies
a *descent* of in-laws	an *overcharge* of plumbers
a *fraid* of ghosts	a *failing* of students
an *innuendo* of gossips	a *slew* of dragons

How Nouns Become Possessive

We have seen that when we pluralise most nouns, we add an -*s* (*ghost*, *ghosts*). Note, no apostrophe. But when a noun changes to its possessive form, we add an -'*s*. Note the apostrophe:

a *ghost*	a *ghost's* shroud
the *team*	the *team's* triumph

Where common nouns end with -*s* (*girls*) we add an apostrophe; with proper nouns we have the option of adding -'*s* as usual, or simply adding an apostrophe after the -*s*:

> The invitation went out for the *girls' party*.
> Instead they went to *James's party* (or *James' party*).

As many of us often find that apostrophe spells catastrophe, there is a more detailed session on the 'upstairs comma' in **Punctuation: What's the Point?** on page 83.

You, I, Me, and Other Pronouns

As we saw in the chapter on **Building Blocks of Sentences**, pronouns are versatile substitutes for nouns and noun phrases. We also noted that they spread like a rash through our speech yet at the same time have the capacity to cause us lots of problems. But before we worry about the dangers, let's find out what pronouns are.

Although perhaps academic, it's worth running through the various kinds of pronouns to see what they do:

PERSONAL PRONOUNS   We use these to identify ourselves and others, and we use them constantly. They are used in three ways:

- In the *first person*, the most intimate, which includes the person or persons doing the speaking or writing: *I*, *me*, *we*, *us*, *myself*, *ourselves*
- In the *second person*, which embraces those who are being addressed: *you*, *yourself*, *yourselves*
- In the *third person*, or 'all the others': *he*, *him*, *she*, *her*, *it*, *they*, *them*, *themselves*, *itself*

With the exception of *it*, which refers to things (and sometimes babies and animals), all personal pronouns refer to people, while *them* can refer to people or things. There are odd exceptions: a ship is not an *it*, but a *she*, or a *her*.

POSSESSIVE PRONOUNS   These indicate possession or ownership and are sometimes called possessive adjectives. Some are used as determiners, and are dependent on nouns:

my groceries, *her* hairdresser, *his* anger, *our* house, *your* car, *their* washing machine

The other possessive pronouns are used on their own:

it is *ours*, it is *mine*, *theirs* is out of date, *his* is that one there, *hers* is over there

REFLEXIVE PRONOUNS   This tribe insinuates its members into our lives in various ways: *Look after yourself*; *they keep to themselves*. Others are *itself*, *herself*, *himself*, *yourselves*, *myself*, *ourselves*.

DEMONSTRATIVE PRONOUNS   These help us to demonstrate something or to point to things:

> I'll take *this*. I'll have *that*.
> *These* will do. *Those* are too stale.

INTERROGATIVE PRONOUNS   These are used to ask questions: *who, what, which, whom, whose*. When you use them, make sure they are followed by a question mark:

> *Who? Who* is she? *Which* one? *Whose* are those?

RELATIVE PRONOUNS   These are *that, which, who, whom* and *whose* and we use them to introduce relative clauses, as in '*It was Claire who asked me first*'. We use them constantly and, with some exceptions, with confidence:

> The suit *that he was supposed to mend* is ruined.
> I wish I knew *whose parcels were damaged*.
> I'd like those shoes *which I saw yesterday*.
> She's the lady *to whom I gave the keys*.

You can see the traps looming, can't you? Taking the last example, many of us would avoid the formal *whom*, and say something like, '*She's the lady I gave the keys to.*' And we are increasingly dropping *that* and *which* from sentences, so that the first and third examples would customarily sound like:

> *The suit he was supposed to mend is ruined.*
> *I'd like those shoes I saw yesterday.*

INDEFINITE PRONOUNS   This is a mixed bunch, but when you see them you will immediately spot a common bond:

> *all, any, every, each, some, one, both, either, neither,*
> *few, little, less, least, many, everyone, someone,*
> *no one, something, anybody, more, most*

They all have to do with quantity: nothing at all, a little, some, or a lot. Here are a few pointers on their use:

- Note that *no one* is the only two-word pronoun
- Note that *little*, *less* and *much* should refer to uncountable nouns (a *little sugar,* but not a *little cakes*; *much trouble*, but not *much problems*; *less fat*, not *less calories*). (See **Twenty Sore Points**, page 96)
- Note that *each*, *one*, *either*, *neither*, *someone*, *no one*, *something* and *anybody* are all singular

When Using Pronouns . . .

A common piece of advice is not to use pronouns without first introducing the nouns they represent, although in practice it's done all the time:

> *It*'s very difficult, *this job*. *Here* it comes! (*the bus*)

Try to avoid using a pronoun when it results in confusion and ambiguity. It is difficult to resist bringing out the old chestnut, 'If your *baby* has trouble digesting cow's milk, boil *it*.'

While pronouns referring to people are of either gender (*he*, *she*) or unspecified (*I*, *me*, *they*) there is an historical propensity to use masculine pronouns to refer to both sexes:

> Any runner who does not finish will have *his* application for next year's race reconsidered by the committee.

What does one do in this age of gender equality? One way is to use the '*his and her*' formula (Any runner who does not finish will have *his* or *her* application . . .) but this is obviously clumsy. A better way is to pluralise the sentence (Runners who do not finish will have *their* applications . . .)

The Business of Verbs

The business of verbs is to express action or to indicate a condition or a state:

ACTION   He *is running* away.
STATE   She *loathes* rap music.

Verbs also help us to express time:

PAST   He*'s been sacked*.
PRESENT   He is *listening* to her sing.
FUTURE   I *will come* if I *can*.

Verbs are among the most versatile of all our words. You can see how brilliant they are in these two paragraphs. The first is a fairly matter-of-fact description:

Then the helicopter banked and almost stalled. The engines roared and the craft tilted and a body fell out of the hatch. The machine rapidly lost height and the engines died. Now only the wind could be heard. Then it began to revolve, falling out of control, throwing Kippy off and finally plunging into the sea.

That could have been a report of a helicopter accident at sea by an aviation safety officer. Here, now, is the same passage, but brought graphically to life by selective verbs:

Suddenly the helicopter banked, shuddered, and seemed to stall, its arms rotating wildly, scrabbling and clawing the black sky for something to grip. The engines whined and screamed and the craft lurched and a body shot out of the hatch and hurtled past Kippy into the void below. The machine was now losing height, dropping at an increasing rate until the engines abruptly died, their howling replaced by the eerie whistling of the wind. Then, slowly at first, the fuselage itself began to spin around the almost stationary rotors, gyrating faster and faster, whirling and spinning out of control, spiralling down through the tunnel of rushing air until, a few seconds after Kippy was hurled off by the force of the spin, the rotors disintegrated and the grey coffin plummeted into the wild black water.

You can easily see how certain verbs – *shuddered*, *rotating*, *scrabbling*, *clawing*, *whined*, *screamed*, *shot*, *hurtled*, *dropping*, *spin*, *gyrating*, *spiralling*, *hurled*, *disintegrated*, *plummeted* – contribute to this vivid, action-packed word picture. To heighten the effect even more, some novelists might move the verbs to the present tense, to give the reader the 'you are there now' feeling:

. . . then, slowly at first, the fuselage itself begins to spin . . . the rotors disintegrate and the grey coffin plummets into the wild black water.

Because verbs are so versatile, it's well worth finding out what they can do, and how you can put them to work. Whole books have been written about verbs (*The English Verb* by Michael Lewis, Language Teaching Publications, 1986, is just one) so this little introduction will merely brush the high spots; nevertheless, they will be the *important* high spots.

Regular and Irregular Verbs

Verbs are divided into two groups, regular, or weak verbs, of which there are thousands, and slightly fewer than 300 irregular, or strong verbs. Regular verbs are so named because they stick to certain rules, while irregular verbs are real wild cards, as you will see.

REGULAR VERBS	*laugh, look, advises, play, loved*
IRREGULAR VERBS	*begin, chosen, speak, froze, shrink*

The difference between these two groups is in their behaviour when they change to express time: present and past time. **Regular** verbs follow a pattern; the basic form of the verb simply adds an *-s*, *-ing*, or *-ed* to express a different person, time or mood:

BASIC FORM	*laugh, look, play, advise, push*
PAST TENSE	*laughed, looked, played, advised, pushed*
PARTICIPLE FORMS (PRESENT)	*laughs, looks, plays, advises, pushes laughing, looking, playing, advising, pushing*

Irregular verbs, however, can behave quite erratically:

PRESENT	*begin, choose, speak, freeze, shrink*
PAST TENSE	*began, chose, spoke, froze, shrank*
PARTICIPLE FORMS (PAST)	*begun, chosen, spoken, frozen, shrunk*

It's the irregular verbs that can give us trouble because they change in such unexpected ways. Some verbs have more than three forms; *be* has eight. It can be most confusing:

> The verse we write we say is written,
> All rules despite, but not despitten,
> And the gas we light is never litten.
> The things we drank were doubtless drunk,
> The boy that's spanked is never spunk,
> The friend we thank is never thunk.
> Suppose we speak, then we have spoken,
> But if we sneak, we have not snoken,
> And shoes that squeak have never squoken.
> The dog that bites has certainly bitten,
> But when it fights, it has not fitten.

As a matter of fact, we conjugate verbs (for that is what this process is called) more or less instinctively and quite successfully ninety-eight per cent of the time, and tend to avoid the few oddniks among irregular verbs that trip us up. But if you would like to master these, you'll find a list of the more obstreperous of them at the end of this chapter.

Other Kinds of Verbs

The verbs discussed so far, whether regular or irregular, are all main verbs. Sometimes, however, they need help from auxiliary verbs to describe subtleties of action.

Auxiliary Verbs

There are two kinds of these: the three primary auxiliaries (*be*, *do*, *have*) which sometimes double as main verbs; and what are known as modal auxiliaries (*can/could*, *may/might*, *must*, *shall/should*, *will/would*) which enable us to express an amazing range of meanings: whether or not something is possible; making demands; giving permission; deducing or predicting some event, and so forth. Also, by following an auxiliary with *not*, we can express a negative. Let's track the main verb *speak* through a range of possibilities:

I speak	I do not speak
she speaks	she does not speak
she is speaking	she is not speaking
she has spoken	she has not spoken
she has been speaking	she has not been speaking
she spoke	she did not speak
she was speaking	she was not speaking
she had spoken	she had not spoken
she had been speaking	she had not been speaking
she will speak	she will not speak

she will be speaking	she will not be speaking
she will have spoken	she will not have spoken
she will have been speaking	she will not have been speaking
she would speak	she would not speak
she would be speaking	she would not be speaking
she would have spoken	she would not have spoken
she would have been speaking	she would not have been speaking
she could speak	she could not speak
she could be speaking	she could not be speaking
she could have spoken	she could not have spoken
etc, etc	

To all these variations you can add a *must speak*, *may speak*, *might speak*, *can speak* and a *shall speak* series. Further, there are several 'fringe' modals that we can trot out to contribute other possibilities: *ought to speak*, *used to speak*, *dare she speak?*, *need she speak?*; plus idiomatic modals such as *had better speak*, *would rather speak* and *has got to speak* (try working backwards from *he's got to be joking!*). It's astonishing, isn't it? It surely demonstrates how verbs, aided by their auxiliaries and a three-letter negative, can offer us so many fine shades of meaning with such economy.

Transitive and Intransitive Verbs

The distinction here is that an intransitive verb can stand alone:

She *speaks*   He *runs*   I *smile*

while nearly all transitive verbs won't work unless they have some sort of relationship:

He *raised* his fist.
She *laid* the book on the bed.

Phrasal Verbs

These are multi-word verbs that incorporate prepositions or adverbs, and they are an interesting lot:

> *look up, look out, look after, look for, give up, take off, break even, called up, look forward to, listen to, fall out, turn down, run up*

You will immediately see that all these examples have an idiomatic feel about them; they are the sort of expressions that pepper our speech.

If we hear someone say 'She loves to *run down* her neighbours', we don't jump to the conclusion that she's trying to kill them with her car. The same applies to 'Will you *run up* a pair of curtains for me?' Why do we *bring up* and not *bring down* a problem? When someone *turns up*, what is that person doing, literally? Or to *go back* on a promise, *chat up* a girl, *turn down* an offer, *put up* with a situation?

Most phrasal verbs do acquire precise meanings:

> He *checked* the speedometer.
> She *checked up* on her husband.

Many phrasal verbs seem to add nothing except paradox to the original verb (*shout down, settle up, ring up*) but not even dynamite will stop us from using them.

Verbless Clauses and Sentences

Verbs are so versatile they can disappear altogether in clauses and even sentences. These are not so much aimless fragments as idiomatic expressions or deliberate constructions for effect:

> *Why all the fuss?*   *What brilliant tennis!*
> *Another glass of*   *Nuts!*
> *wine?*

Having begun this chapter with a paragraph loaded with verbs and concluded it with no verbs at all, one item remains, and that is the list of verbal tripwires promised earlier:

Those Disorderly, Disobedient, Deviating Irregular Verbs

Present	Past	Past Participle
arise	arose	arisen
awake	awoke	awoken
be	was	been
bear	bore	borne
bid	bad	bidden
bite	bit	bitten
burn	burned/burnt	burned/burnt
burst	burst	burst
choose	chose	chosen
dive	dived	dived
do	did	done
drive	drove	driven
forgive	forgave	forgiven
go	went	gone
hang	hung/hanged	hung/hanged
kneel	kneeled/knelt	knelt/kneeled
lay	laid	laid
lean	leaned/leant	leant/leaned
lie	lay	lain
mistake	mistook	mistaken
mow	mowed	mown
quit	quit/quitted	quit/quitted
rid	rid	rid
saw	sawed	sawn
sew	sewed	sewn

Present	Past	Past Participle
shear	sheared	shorn/sheared
shoe	shoed/shod	shod
show	showed	shown/showed
slay	slew	slain
smell	smelled/smelt	smelt/smelled
speed	speeded/sped	sped/speeded
spell	spelled/spelt	spelt/spelled
spin	span/spun	spun
spring	sprang	sprung
steal	stole	stolen
stink	stank	stunk
strew	strewed	strewn
stride	strode	stridden/strode
strike	struck	stricken/struck
strive	strove	striven
swell	swelled	swollen
teach	taught	taught
thrive	thrived/throve	thrived/thriven
tread	trod	trodden/trod
undergo	underwent	undergone
undertake	undertaken	undertook
undo	undid	undone
wake	waked/woke	woken/waked
weave	wove	woven
wet	wet/wetted	wet/wetted
wring	wrung	wrung

Describing Things —
Adjectives and Adverbs

Adjectives define and modify nouns while adverbs do the same for nouns and verbs. They are close relations in a very big family of words, and often are difficult to tell apart; so that when we use them we sometimes misuse or abuse them. It's therefore useful to know something about adjectives and adverbs and how we can use them to better effect.

Here's a sentence in which the meaning depends almost entirely on adjectives and adverbs:

You're buying the	*best,*	ADJECTIVE
	most	ADVERB
	expensive,	ADJECTIVE
	exciting	PARTICIPLE
and	*arguably*	ADVERB
highest	*performance*	ADJECTIVE/NOUN
	saloon	NOUN/ADJECTIVE
	car	NOUN

There are four kinds of modifier in this sentence: several adjectives, two adverbs, a participle (the verb *excite* turned into an adjective by adding *-ing*, discussed in the next chapter), and two nouns (*performance*, *saloon*) that are used in an adjectival way.

Writing a sentence like that is a bit like juggling four balls, but most of us manage to do it tolerably well without too many mishaps.

In the chapter on *Parts of Speech* we found that we could identify many adverbs by their *-ly* endings. That's fine for adverbs with *-ly* endings, but there are many without, and there are also some adjectives with *-ly* endings. It is these that cause confusion:

ADJECTIVES	ADVERBS
He is a *slow* driver.	He drives *slowly*.
She is an *early* riser.	She rises *early*.

That's very *loud* music.	He's playing *loudly*.
It was a *straight* road.	She drove *straight* home.
He read a *daily* newspaper.	He reads a paper *daily*.

Obviously we must be wary of adjectives and adverbs that don't play by the rules. We've all seen signs that say: *GO SLOW!* and wonder, on reflection, if it ought to say, *GO SLOWLY!* Our reason is that *slow* in *SLOW LANE* is an adjective, *slowly* (by its suffix *-ly*) is an adverb, therefore it should be the latter. Correct; but in this case, modern usage allows both *slow* and *slowly*. The following examples, however, are still regarded as bad news:

She put her lips to his ear and spoke *soft*. *(softly)*
I'm afraid I've let him down *bad*. *(badly)*
That feels *real* great! *(really)*

You are excused if some confusion still exists, which is all the more reason why we should subject both adjectives and adverbs to some closer study.

Adjectives

Here are some adjectives in use to show you how free-ranging they are:

DESCRIBING SIZE	It was a *huge* marquee.
DESCRIBING COLOUR	The carpet was *red*.
DESCRIBING A QUALITY	I loved the *plush* armchairs.
DEFINING QUANTITY	There were *five* windows.
DEFINING SPECIFICITY	Did you see her *Persian* rug?
. . . and so on	

Adjectives can come before a noun (*huge marquee*) and after a number of verbs: the *be* family – *is, are, was, were, am, being, been; look, seem, become, stay*, etc (carpet *was* red). They can 'top and tail' a sentence
64

(*Welsh* singing is world *famous*), follow nouns (he requested that all the journalists *present* should leave) and pronouns (did you find anything *useful*?). And of course they can be used liberally:

> What impressed her most of all were the *three big ancient green-tinged metallic Burmese religious* figures.

A bit over the top, but here we have no less than seven adjectives all adding something to the description of the figures. It's worth noting that, although no strict rules exist to tell you in which order your adjectives should be, it should follow a common-sense sequence. For example, you know immediately that something's wrong here:

> What impressed her most of all were the *Burmese religious three big green-tinged ancient metallic* figures.

An acceptable rule-of-thumb for arranging your adjectives is:

QUANTITY	*five, a hundred*
EMOTIVE	*lovely, ugly, rare*
SIZE	*large, tiny*
AGE	*brand new, old*
COLOUR, TEXTURE	*ochreous, blue, smooth*
SPECIFICITY	*Jewish, Japanese, Xeroxed*
PURPOSE	*dining* table, *wine* glass

which, followed to the letter, might result in something like this:

> The catalogue listed *two exquisite 23in. 18th century Peruzzi silver candle* sticks.

Recognising Adjectives

What makes an adjective? Many of them are original descriptive words like *good*, *dark*, *hot* and *rough*, many of which have their opposites: *bad*, *fair*, *cold* and *smooth*. But thousands more began life as nouns and verbs and were changed into adjectives by having endings tacked on to them. These are fairly easy to recognise as adjectives:

-able	*notable, fashionable, detestable, desirable*
-ible	*sensible, comprehensible, horrible, responsible*
-al	*natural, mortal, skeletal, oriental*
-ar	*jocular, circular, spectacular, singular*
-ed	*excited, crooked, married, cracked*
-ent	*excellent, indulgent, emergent, deficient*
-esque	*picturesque, Romanesque, statuesque*
-ful	*wonderful, hopeful, forgetful, thoughtful*
-ic	*heroic, psychic, angelic, romantic*
-ical	*periodical, magical, farcical, psychological*
-ish	*liverish, childish, quirkish, British*
-ive	*reflective, massive, defensive, offensive*
-less	*endless, cloudless, hopeless, legless*
-like	*lifelike, ladylike, childlike*
-ous	*nervous, herbaceous, piteous, officious*
-some	*meddlesome, awesome, loathsome, fearsome*
-worthy	*newsworthy, praiseworthy, seaworthy*

and two endings to watch for:

-ly	*lonely, crinkly, sickly, prickly*
-y	*earthy, shaky, funny, tacky, kinky*

These two endings provide a wildly (adverb) frothing bubbly (adjective) brew of pitfalls and booby traps. Try to separate the adjectives from the adverbs:

truly idly gravelly loyally woolly yearly holy thankfully gentlemanly brazenly properly

If you try placing each of the words before a noun (truly car, gravelly voice) you should score 100%. The adjectives are gravelly, woolly, yearly, holy and gentlemanly; the rest are adverbs.

Kinds of Adjectives

You must be aware now that adjectives cover a lot of ground. Even possessive pronouns like *many*, *this*, *my*, *his* and *her* can be used as adjectives. There are adjectives which can rove around a sentence with some freedom, and others that are locked into certain positions. The former are called central adjectives, and the latter are peripheral adjectives:

CENTRAL ADJECTIVE	This is a *new* car.
	This car is *new*.
	New the car may be, but it is far too expensive.
PERIPHERAL ADJECTIVE	The man spoke *utter* nonsense.

Here you can see that *utter* cannot be moved to any other position (*The man spoke nonsense that was utter?*); its function here as an adjective is specifically to qualify the noun *nonsense*. For different degrees of nonsense we might have used adjectives like *absolute*, *puerile* or *childish*, but in this case the old cliché does an effective job.

In an earlier example, we saw *Welsh* used as an adjective, and noted that *British* is also an adjective. These are called proper adjectives (*Chippendale* furniture, *Shrewsbury* cake) because they define a particular thing; common adjectives describe classes of things: *leafy* tree, *white* house, *angry* bull.

The Expanding Adjective

One of the most valuable services adjectives provide is a range of comparisons. Imagine trying to describe the comparative sizes of three bundles of ten-pound notes without having recourse to the words *small/smaller/smallest* and *large/larger/largest*. Most adjectives work like that; they can express several comparative elements: the same, less, least, more, most. In some cases we add *-er* (*taller, weaker*) or *-est* (*tallest, weakest*); while in others we qualify the adjective with *more* (*more entertaining*); *most* (*most endearing*); *less* (*less enthusiastic*) or *least* (the *least likely*). All these adjectival devices enable us to describe almost anything, any action, any feeling, with extraordinary accuracy:

> It was a *big* celebration. It was a *very big*
> celebration. It was the *biggest* celebration ever.
> It was *bigger* than any other celebration I've seen.
> It was a *fairly big* celebration. It was *quite a big*
> celebration. Well, it was a *biggish* celebration . . .

etc etc. Then we can move on to *huge*, *vast* and *gargantuan*!

Tips on Using Adjectives

● BE AWARE OF CLICHÉ ADJECTIVES   These are what the novelist and columnist Keith Waterhouse calls 'limpet adjectives' – they always seem to stick to certain nouns:

widespread concern	*drastic steps*	*utmost urgency*
long-felt want	*true facts*	*full inquiry*

● AVOID REPETITIOUS ADJECTIVES   The definition of the word *history* is 'a record of past events', so why do we so often read a sentence like, '*The disagreement is now past history*'? Sloppiness or ignorance is the answer, and redundancy (or pleonasm, as grammarians have it) is the problem.

Here are some typical examples:

> *personal* friend *unexpected* surprise
> *amazing* miracle *actual* fact *mobile* van
> *wet* puddle a *warm* 28 degrees *tall* skyscraper

● PRACTICE ADJECTIVAL ECONOMY To demonstrate the use of adjectives, an earlier example used a pile-up of seven of them, which is rather too many. Overloads of this sort cause confusion; by the time the reader has reached the last one the first is probably forgotten. If you find you've written a sentence with more than half a dozen adjectives, try another construction. Furthermore, make sure that every adjective you use adds something essential to the sentence: 'Her skis sliced through the *powdery white* snow on her *downward* trajectory'. Most of us know that snow is white, and believe that it is difficult to ski uphill, so the adjectives *white* and *downward* could well be returned to the dictionary.

Adverbs

As with adjectives, we use adverbs to add information and extra layers of meaning to a statement. Adverbs, however, are far more versatile; while adjectives can dress up nouns and pronouns, adverbs are regular Houdinis, modifying a verb here, boosting an adjective there, appearing in disguise to support another adverb – even bossing phrases and whole sentences about! And as we have seen, they disguise themselves so well sometimes that they can be mistaken for adjectives:

ADVERBS   The train arrived *early*. She hadn't *long* left home.

ADJECTIVES   They caught the *early* train. He drew a *long* line.

How Adverbs Work

Here is a short catalogue of how we can use adverbs to add information and meaning:

DEFINE MANNER	They played *happily* together.
DENOTE PLACE	They can play over *there*.
FIX TIME	We can all go there *afterwards*.
EXPRESS GRADATION	We never seem to see *enough*.
EXPRESS FREQUENCY	We *hardly ever* go there.
INDICATE VIEWPOINT	I would never go there, *personally*.
LINK TO A PREVIOUS THOUGHT	*Nevertheless*, I feel we should go.
INDICATE ATTITUDE	*Curiously*, she has never been there.

You will note that while many adverbs are stand-alone words like *there*, *enough*, *up*, *now*, *here*, *very*, etc., others have been created from existing words. The most common of these constructions is the *-ly* suffix (*personally*, *curiously*, *romantically*, *historically*); other suffixes include *-wise* (*clockwise*, *otherwise*); *-wards* (*backwards*, *homewards*); and *-ways* (*endways*, *always*).

Enough? (That's an exclamatory adverb, used as a sentence.) There is little reason to dwell on the detailed workings of adverbs like those above, because from childhood we've learned to handle them with intuitive assurance.

What is worth looking into, however, is the order in which adverbs should appear in a sentence. Because of their versatility, adverbs offer a lot of options. In his book *Rediscover Grammar*, David Crystal demonstrates this all-purpose quality with devastating effect, using a seven-way sentence:

1. *Originally*, the book must have been bought in the shop.
2. The book *originally* must have been bought in the shop.

3. The book must *originally* have been bought in the shop.
4. The book must have *originally* been bought in the shop.
5. The book must have been *originally* bought in the shop.
6. The book must have been bought *originally* in the shop.
7. The book must have been bought in the shop, *originally*.

Positioning Your Adverbs

Not all adverbs are so adaptable, however; most feel uncomfortable in certain positions while others, wrongly placed, can produce ambiguity and even hilarity. This rough guide should make you aware of such adverbial problems:

DEFINING MANNER:	adverb usually towards end of sentence
Not advised –	He rather *erratically* walked.
Much better –	He walked rather *erratically*.
DENOTING PLACE:	adverb typically towards end of sentence
Not advised –	Over *there* he threw the stone.
Much better –	He threw the stone over *there*.
FIXING TIME:	adverb best towards end of sentence
Not advised –	I *recently* saw that film.
Much better –	I saw that film *recently*.
EXPRESSING GRADATION:	adverb works best in the middle

Not advised –	The jar is full, *almost*.
Much better –	The jar is *almost* full.
INDICATING FREQUENCY:	adverb usually not at beginning
Not advised –	*Always* he is going to the pub.
Much better –	He is *always* going to the pub.
DENOTING ATTITUDE:	most effective at the front of a sentence
Not advised –	They both decided to *wisely* stay away.
Much better –	*Wisely*, they both decided to stay away.
INDICATING VIEWPOINT:	again, best placed at the front
Not advised –	I shouldn't comment, *strictly speaking*.
Much better –	*Strictly speaking*, I shouldn't comment.

Keep in mind that a guide such as this is not a rule book, for there are many exceptions. *Enough* is an adverb of gradation or degree and it is commonly placed in the middle of a sentence: *I've done enough work for today*. But look what happens when enough is placed at the end or beginning of a sentence: *Do you think they've had enough? Enough has been said on the subject of adverbs!* What has happened is that in these two examples, *enough* has turned into a noun. Look at the sentences again and you will see that this is so.

One of the most contentious adverbial placements is known as the split infinitive in which, typically, an adverb or adverbial phrase finds its way between the preposition *to* and a basic verb form:

    to dearly love   to properly understand   to boldly go

This really isn't an issue any more, and many modern

grammarians will happily provide you with a nickel-plated infinitive-splitter to use to your heart's content. It is discussed in some detail in **Twenty Sore Points** on page 100.

Some Tips on Using Adverbs

• BEWARE OF MISPLACED ADVERBS Always keep adverbs like *nearly*, *only*, *even*, *quite*, *just*, etc, as near as possible to the words they're meant to modify. *He just went to the store to buy some jeans* could mean that very recently he went to the store to buy jeans; what the writer meant was, *He went to the store* just *to buy some jeans*.

• BE WARY OF STARTING SENTENCES WITH ADVERBS *Interestingly*, this advice is given by *The Times* to its journalists; this sentence is an example. 'Such constructions,' advises *The Times*, 'are not forbidden, but sentences starting with adverbs are normally built on sand.'

• AVOID 'NEUTRALISING' ADVERBS Such phrases as *faintly repulsive*, *rather appalling*, *pretty meaningless*, *somewhat threatening* and *slightly lethal* cancel out the intended effect. Such an oxymoronic habit should be *gently stamped out*.

Grammatical Glue

This is something of a 'bits and pieces' chapter about those grammatical elements you remember vaguely but whose exact function you can't recall: determiners, conjunctions, prepositions and participles. When you see these terms translated into words you'll see how important they are:

DETERMINERS	*a, the, this, my, which, all*
CONJUNCTIONS	*and, but, or, if, because, like, whereas*
PREPOSITIONS	*with, at, to, for, on, in, around*
PARTICIPLES	*reading, growing, knocked, worked* and many thousands of words ending in *-ing* and *-ed*

Together, these words and their companions form a mass of grammatical glue with which we construct all our writing and speech. It is simply impossible to communicate without this glue. If anyone should attempt even a short passage of English without it, the passage might look like this:

> Windows room were wide open, Paris immense level abyss that itself foot house, built perpendicularly hill. Helene, out long chair, was windows.

It's a bit like one of those model kits in which all the pieces are present but none of it makes sense until you stick them all together. Here's the paragraph assembled and glued:

> Both windows of the room were wide open, and Paris unfolded its immense level in the abyss that hollowed itself at the foot of the house, built perpendicularly on the hill. Helene, stretched out on her long chair, was reading at one of the windows.

Obviously, we should know more about this useful stuff.

Determiners

Quite simply, determiners precede and determine certain qualities of nouns and noun phrases. In the attributive sense, they act as adjectives. Here, for example, is a partial list of the determiners we use most. The first four kinds are used to indicate that the noun is personal or specific, and are called *Definites*:

DEFINITE ARTICLE	I will buy *the* car. / He will see *the* car.
POSSESSIVE	It is *my* car. / It is *his* car.
POSSESSIVE PROPER	It is *Fred's* car. / It is *Lyn's* car.
DEMONSTRATIVE	I want *that* car. / He bought *this* car.
NUMBER	You have *two* cars? / No, just *one* car.

The next group of determiners are called *Indefinites* because they generalise or broadly qualify nouns:

INDEFINITE ARTICLE	I saw *a* great movie. / She ate *an* apple.
QUANTIFIER	She saw *every* movie. / I saw *most* movies.
EXCLAMATORY	*What* a movie! / It was *such* a great movie!
INTERROGATIVE	*What* movie? / *Whose* ticket did you use?

Once again, we find that we possess an easy familiarity with such words. We know not to use two determiners together: *I will buy the a car. Did you see some several movies?* We also learn to drop following nouns: *I saw them all* [movies]. *I bought both* [cars]. With ear and instinct most of us experience very few problems with determiners.

Conjunctions

Conjunctions are very strong glue because we use them to link parts of sentences together:

> She plays the violin *and* also the piano.

In this example, *and* is the conjunction that co-ordinates both parts of the sentence. It is the simplest kind of conjunction in that it is a link and nothing more; it adds nothing new to the sentence. In fact, you could turn it right round without altering the meaning:

> She plays the piano *and* also the violin.

But there are other conjunctions that, while gluing a sentence together, can also impart extra meaning:

> She likes the piano, *but* the violin is her favourite.

You'll note that this is not the same as *She likes the piano and the violin is her favourite*; the conjunction *but* promises an exception or a contrast. *And* is bland; *but*, *either/or*, *neither/nor* and *yet* offer more possibilities; but the strongest and most versatile conjunctions are the Subordinators. These conjunctions can provide quite a lot of information while still doing their joining job.

They are usually grouped according to the meaning they add to the join:

Expressing	Some examples	Typical usage
Time	*before, after, till, until, since, as soon as, while*	She'll come home *after* she's finished.
Place	*where, wherever*	I'll find out *where* he comes from.
Cause	*since, because, as, for*	I feel ill *because* I ate too much.
Condition	*if, although, unless, or, as long as*	I'll feel better *if* I lie down.
Comparison	*as, than, like, as if, as though*	It looks *like* it will rain.
Contrast	*although, while, whereas*	I'm good at English *while* she's good at maths.
Purpose	*so that, so as to, lest, in order that*	I must stop *so as to* allow others to speak.
Result	*so, so that, such that*	He shouted *so that* they could hear him.
Preference	*sooner than, rather than*	I'd eat worms *rather than* go hungry.
Exception	*except, except that, excepting that*	He'd play, *except that* he's torn a muscle.

Apart from this wide choice of hard-working conjunctions you can also dip into what are sometimes described as 'disguised conjunctions' like *considering*, *owing to*, *barring*, *provided* and *including*. These were formerly participles, which we'll look at after considering prepositions.

Prepositions – and Where to Put Them

About the only thing most of us know about prepositions is that they should never be used to end a sentence with! But this old rule hardly exists nowadays; instead, we are encouraged to use our own judgement on how we should end our sentences. But more of that later. Of greater importance is mastering the subtleties of this irksome but indispensable group of words.

A preposition usually acts as a linking word, like a conjunction, but it also relates one part of a sentence to the other:

We went	*to*	the beach.
She rose	*at*	dawn.

From just these two examples you will have noticed that prepositions have a particular ability to unite two elements in terms of space (*to*) and time (*at*). To clarify this point, here are some common prepositions:

SPACE	*between, above, over, into, near, beside, along*
TIME	*until, since, past, before, after, at, during*
OTHERS	*as, for, in, to, but, by, with, without*
MULTI-WORD	*instead of, other than, in front of, up to*

An interesting thing about prepositions is that when you use one in a sentence, it can only be replaced by another preposition:

She found a mouse *in* the house.
She found a mouse *near* the house.

She found a mouse *under* the house.

. . . and so on. You could substitute any number of prepositions – *beside*, *inside* – but only with some difficulty could you substitute any other class of words, say, adjectives, adverbs, determiners, conjunctions, nouns or verbs. You might say that a preposition is like a keystone in an arch; take it away, and . . .

There are really only three problems with prepositions. The first is that we tend to create long-winded ones when quite adequate short ones are freely available. In his *The Complete Plain Words*, Sir Ernest Gowers refers to these as verbose prepositions, and gives a list of them together with simpler equivalents. Here are a few worth avoiding:

as a consequence of (*because of*)
in the course of (*during*)
in excess of (*more than*)
for the purpose of (*to*)
for the reason that (*because*)
in the neighbourhood of (*about*)
in the nature of (*like*)
in addition to (*besides*)
with a view to (*to*)
in case of (*if*)
prior to (*before*)
subsequent to (*after*)
in order to (*to*)
in the event of (*if*)

The second problem with prepositions is the one already referred to. That is, like the last sentence, allowing a sentence to end with a preposition. A preposition pedant would have written, 'The second problem with prepositions is the one to which we've already referred.'

The reason for the objection can be traced back to the influence of Latin grammar on English; in Latin, ending a sentence with a preposition was frowned upon.

Generations of scholars upheld the rule, although when masters of the language like Shakespeare (In *Hamlet*: 'No traveller returns, puzzles the will,/ And makes us rather bear those ills we have / Then fly to others that we know not of?') started hanging them out to dry, the big rethink on prepositions began. The modern view is that unless they send jarring notes to the ear, let them stay. A sentence like, *That's the restaurant we ate in,* is perfectly acceptable. Quite often, extremely clumsy sentences result from straining to avoid finishing with a preposition; demonstrated neatly by Winston Churchill when, criticising some civil servant's prose, he commented, 'This is the sort of English up with which I will not put.' What we should be concentrating on, instead, is which prepositions should follow certain words. For example:

Do you	aim *for*	or	aim *at?*
Is it	disgust *over*	or	disgust *for?*
Is it	superior *than*	or	superior *to?*
Are you	oblivious *to*	or	oblivious *of?*

According to the great grammarian Eric Partridge, the latter choice is the correct usage. And there are dozens more; far too many to be listed here.

The third problem with prepositions is that the lazier among us tend to drop them altogether:

> Defenestration means throwing someone out the window.

should read, *out of the window.* It is, needless to say, a habit to be discouraged.

Participles – Misplaced and Dangling

Participles are forms of verbs:

> The horse *is galloping.*

The orchestra *is playing*.

When they are used to modify nouns they act like adjectives, as in *galloping inflation*. You can also see that the two examples above – *galloping* and *playing* – are simply verbs with *-ing* added. That's one form of participle, indicating the present, but there is another, indicating past tenses:

PRESENT add *ing*   *travelling, falling, telling, swimming*

PAST add *-ed*, *-en*, etc   *travelled, fallen, told, swum*

Here are some examples of a participle in use:

> *Travelling* back from Italy, she stopped in Paris.
> They *have travelled* constantly, staying at hotels.
> *Having travelled* for miles, he was tired and dirty.

Using participles like this adds interest and elegance to sentences. They are deceptively easy to use and we tend to launch them into our written and spoken sentences without so much as a thought. And that is the trouble, for every now and then we crash, brought down by a dangler.

Danglers and Manglers

- The exhibition features works by fashion photographers executed between 1940 and 1990.
- Being not yet fully grown, his trousers were too long.
- After descending through the clouds, London lay beneath us.
- If Swallowed, Seek Medical Advice. (poison label)

What's wrong with these sentences? What's wrong is that they have all been brought crashing down by danglers – dangling or disconnected participle phrases, participles that have lost their way or lost their noun. The result, in all cases, is ambiguity and even hilarity.

Were the photographers really executed? Of course not. Did London descend from the clouds? Have you ever seen growing trousers? And if you were swallowed, would you be in a condition to seek medical aid?

When this sort of thing happens, some rewriting is called for: (Notice the prepositional ending?)

- The exhibition features fashion photographers' works executed between 1940 and 1990.
- Because he was not yet fully grown, his trousers were too long.
- After we descended through the clouds, London lay beneath us.
- If Contents Are Swallowed, Seek Medical Advice.

The trick is, of course, to make sure that your participle is linked to its correct noun.

Mangled sentences like *Abraham Lincoln wrote the Gettysburg Address while travelling from Washington on the back of an envelope* are perhaps not as common as those habitually beginning with participles like *Speaking candidly* . . .

Speaking as an old friend, there has been a disturbing tendency in statements emanating from Peking . . .

That was former US President Nixon addressing a Chinese trade delegation, which may have wondered who was doing the speaking. What the President should have said is:

Speaking as an old friend, I have noted a disturbing . . .

Use participles by all means, but don't let your danglers do you in.

Punctuation: What's the Point?

Move a comma, as they say, and lose a friend; change a comma and save your life. Those dots, strokes and squiggles may be physically insignificant on the page and evanescent in our speech, but without them all would be chaos. Not knowing how to use them correctly can produce even more chaos. If you were to say to a person,

> I hate hypocrites; like you, I find them detestable.

that person would very likely agree. But imagine the reaction should you monkey slightly with the punctuation:

> I hate hypocrites like you; I find them detestable.

Old-time teachers were fond of quoting this chestnut: KING CHARLES I PRAYED HALF AN HOUR AFTER HE WAS BEHEADED. 'Jones at the back, there – where should the dot go?' Another well-known illustration recounts the fate of a warrior in ancient Greece who, on the eve of leaving for a war, visits the Oracle at Delphi. *Thou shalt go thou shalt return never by war shalt thou perish*, he was told. Mentally placing the commas after *go* and *return*, he left with great confidence. Unfortunately, he was killed in the first battle without realising that what the Oracle meant was, *Thou shalt go, thou shalt return never, by war shalt thou perish*. Less morbid are those gags that have a lady librarian placing an ad in a newspaper's personal classifieds: *Lonely librarian seeks a man who reads*. But the typesetter garbled the message and it appeared as: *Lonely librarian seeks a man. Who reads?*

> Sentences begin with a capital letter,
> To help you make your writing better.
> Use full stops to mark the end
> Of all the sentences you've penned.

runs an old rhyme. Seems absurdly basic, doesn't it, but you'd be surprised by the number of people who can interpret whole knots of complex road signs while driving at speed but cannot navigate their way through the grammatical equivalents.

Capitals and Stops

'Punctuation', *The Times* advises its journalists, 'is . . . not a fireworks display to show off your dashes and gaspers. Remember the first rule: the best punctuation is the full stop.'

A full stop (or stop, point or period) is used like a knife to cut off a sentence at the required length. The rule is that simple: where you place your stops is up to you, but generally it is at the point where your thought is complete, and the sentence looks and sounds right. When you are ready to embark on another thought, that's the time to think about a full stop. Master this, and you can then move on to using full stops stylistically, for emphasis:

> You couldn't get near Harry all day because he was constantly on the prowl, hunched in his greasy pants and dirty sweater, looking mean and taciturn and with his mind no doubt churning with murderous thoughts, for he had announced to too many people in too many places and in too loud a voice that he would kill Evans the instant he clapped eyes on him. And he did.

Commas

Commas are a little more complicated, perhaps because, although 'listening' to a sentence can be a good guide to comma placement, the pauses they create don't necessarily follow speech patterns. A comma's role is not to act as 'breath pauses' but to separate different thoughts within sentences.

> The snapshot with its naively honest images revolutionised our way of seeing the world.

Because this sentence would make essentially the same statement if it were written as *The snapshot revolutionised our way of seeing the world*, the incidental clause *with its naively honest images* is a relevant but separate thought, and should be separated from the main thrust of the statement by commas:

> The snapshot, with its naively honest images, revolutionised our way of seeing the world.

You'll notice that two commas are required to do this; a common mistake is to drop the second comma.

Here is a selection of typical comma placements:

BETWEEN ADJECTIVES	*It was a brash, garish, ugly painting. It was brash and garish, ugly and sloppy, and also quite worthless.*
BETWEEN VERBS	*He drank, swore, and abruptly departed.*
BETWEEN ADVERBS	*She crept down slowly, nervously, noiselessly, into the dark room.*
BETWEEN PREPOSITIONS	*The experience was for him, as for her, quite devastating.*
BETWEEN CONJUNCTIONS	*They wondered if, because the dogs were loose, they should venture in.*

In the last example you will see that a comma is almost always necessary between two conjunctions: *so that, while . . .; as, since . . .; because, in order that . . .* etc.

Apart from these semi-rules, placing commas is a judgmental matter. The fashion today (grammatical fashions change, albeit over centuries) is to do without them if the meaning remains clear, even to

saying *firm ripe bananas* in lieu of *firm, ripe bananas*.
Despite this, many people still insist on commas that
are decorative but redundant:

> Looking back, to the early days of the war, I
> sometimes think we were lucky.
> To the farmer it is a welcome sight, to see the
> stubble.
> The jay is a bird, that comes into the woods in
> June.

All three sentences would read better if the commas
after *back*, *sight* and *bird* were deleted.

Another common error is the comma used instead of
a linking conjunction to join two sentences:

WRONG   James took the car, it had an almost
        empty tank.
RIGHT   James took the car but it had an almost
        empty tank.

Semicolons

There is something about semicolons that can raise the
blood pressure. The writer George Orwell was so
against them that he wrote one of his novels, *Coming
Up for Air* (1939), without a single semicolon in it.
Actually, three crept in, only to be removed in later
editions. George Bernard Shaw complained of T. E.
Lawrence that while he threw colons about like a
madman he hardly used semicolons at all. Indeed, the
heat provoked by the anti-semicolonists some years ago
led to fears that it would become an endangered
species, and a Society for the Preservation of the
Semicolon was formed.

A semicolon is a pause somewhere between a strong
comma and a weak full stop. It is used to join phrases
and sentences which are related in theme but
independent and which would be disjointed if
86

separated by a full stop. This example by Partridge demonstrates it beautifully:

> If you can possibly do so, come; if you cannot come, write; if you haven't the time to write, send a telegram.

While it is true that semicolons are falling into disuse (from misuse?), they are very useful for joining phrases or sentences without recourse to conjunctions (*and*, *but*, *although*, etc.), and indispensable for separating matter which already contains commas:

> The speakers included Monica Watts, author of *The Autumn Triangle*; David Beardman, columnist, restaurateur and broadcaster; and Peter Tate, professional golfer.

Colons

The legendary grammarian Henry Fowler defined the function of the colon as 'delivering the goods that have been invoiced in the preceding words'. This might take the form of a conclusion, a summary, a list, or a quotation:

> There was one very good reason for his failure: *his right hand never knew what his left was doing.*
> She listened patiently for some minutes before her mind was made up: *she would go to Bath immediately.*
> Detective Stevens entered and took it all in: *the body, the still smouldering mattress, the fallen pipe.*
> Gradually, one by one, the words came back to me: *'And we forget because we must and not because we will.'*

In all four examples you will note that what precedes the colon is an otherwise complete sentence.

One final thought on the colon: It is *not* (like this

one) followed by a capitalised word in the same
paragraph.

Hyphens and Dashes

Except that they are little horizontal lines and one is
shorter than the other, hyphens and dashes are not
closely related. A hyphen joins two or more words
together, while a dash keeps them apart. What they
do have in common is that they are inclined to be
overused and abused.

The rules governing the use of hyphens are probably
the most complex and contradictory in grammar,
which is why their use is increasingly discouraged.
Generally, their chief use nowadays (which used to be
now-a-days) is to avoid ambiguity, and this is the line
we'll follow here.

When To Hyphen and When Not To Hyphen

Here are instances where hyphens are advisable or
unavoidable:

NOUNS AND PARTICIPLES USED AS ADJECTIVES	*hand-reared, bird-brained, weather-beaten, fact-finding*
ADJECTIVES AND PARTICIPLES USED AS ADJECTIVES	*bleary-eyed, good-looking, middle-aged, sour-tasting*
VERBS AND ADVERBS USED AS NOUNS	*passer-by, summing-up, break-in* (but *breakdown*!)
PHRASES USED AS ADJECTIVES	*door-to-door, good-for-nothing, open-air*
PHRASES USED AS NOUNS	*get-together, ne'er-do-well*
SOME PREFIXES	*ex-detective, pre-natal, vice-chancellor*

IDIOMATICS	*T-shirt, X-ray, U-turn*
NUMBERS	*twenty-one, ninety-nine* (but *three hundred and twenty-three*)
TO REDUCE CONFUSION	*re-cover* (if you mean to cover a settee) to avoid confusing with *recover*; *re-create*
LETTER COLLISION	*co-op, shell-like, de-ice*
PREFIXING PROPER NOUNS	*anti-Semitism, ex-British*
FAMILY COMPOUNDS	*mother-in-law, great-grandfather*

Such a catalogue could go on and on, each entry with its list of exceptions. A dictionary is essential to be absolutely sure, but even then some entries will be overtaken by current usage; not so long ago, words like *taxpayer* and *manpower* were hyphenated. When in doubt, leave it out. In his excellent *English Our English*, Keith Waterhouse warned that fruitless hours could be spent pondering hyphenating problems – like whether it should be *second-hand car salesmen* or *second-hand-car salesmen*. The unhyphenated *used car salesmen* seems to be the solution.

Dash It All

Advice on using dashes is rather more straightforward – don't! Or at least, use them sparingly.

Dashes are useful for inserting parenthetical statements into sentences.

> Mrs Owen immediately dived into the broom cupboard – *she was obsessive about crumbs on the*

lino – and emerged with the business end of a
vacuum hose.

Such an aside or observation could have been enclosed
within brackets, but the dashes (one at the beginning,
and don't forget the one at the end) in this case were
probably preferred because of their informality.

While dashes can substitute for colons, they should
not be used in place of commas, which is considered
to be a sign of sloppy writing. Nor should more than
one pair of dashes be used in a sentence. But they can
be effectively used for certain dramatic effects:

> In Hollywood if an actor's wife looks like a new
> woman – she probably is.

Brackets and Parentheses

What's the difference? Some confusion here, but
parentheses usually refers to (round brackets), and
brackets to [square brackets]. The latter are used for
special purposes, so need not concern us. The words
contained within the parentheses or round brackets are
said to be in parenthesis.

Parentheses are discouraged by stylists who would
rather have you reconstruct your sentence using
commas instead. But they are useful for including
explanations, comments and afterthoughts in
sentences:

EXPLANATION   The films of Lloyd Hamilton (born
1891) constitute the bedrock of
cinematic archaeology.

COMMENT   Cruelty to animals (I noted a scene
in which a donkey's tail was tied to
a post, and another where a jam tin
with a firecracker in it was attached
to a dog's tail) was a fairly common
sight in children's comic papers in
the 1920s.

AFTERTHOUGHT Travel by car, choose the cross-channel route that offers best value for money, and look out for bargains (like newspaper tokens. Last summer we scored a free hotel in France).

There are two observations to be made on these examples. In the second example the matter in parenthesis is longer than the rest of the sentence, a situation to avoid. The third example illustrates a common error. Whatever is in parenthesis should be punctuated normally, i.e. as though the parentheses don't exist. Thus the full stop after *France* comes after a complete sentence and therefore should be *inside* the bracket: *Last summer we scored a free hotel in France.*)

Question Marks

Questions require question marks, but indirect questions do not:

DIRECT QUESTION *Can I buy a ticket?*
INDIRECT QUESTION *I asked if I could buy a ticket.*

Generally question marks come at the end of sentences but sometimes should be inserted within them:

Perhaps – who knows? – there may someday be some belated recognition for his services.

Don't forget that, no matter how long your sentence is, if there is a question in it, a question mark is still required:

Is it not curious that *Lourdes*, which within a year of publication sold over 200,000 copies, had critical acclaim poured over it like champagne and which caused such a furore that it was immediately placed on the Vatican's Index of prohibited books, is not still read today?

Exclamation Mark

These are probably the most overused of all grammatical marks, and are often served up in double, and even triple, doses:

> Sylvia went to Rome – again! That's the second time this year!!! And you'll never know who she met there!!

If that example isn't enough to put you off, nothing will. Use them only to express the strongest of feelings, and don't use them to cap jokes.

Quotation Marks

These inverted commas are used to enclose direct quotations and were once known as 'sixty-sixes' and 'ninety-nines' because of their resemblance to 66 and 99. In these days of typographical cleaning-up, however, you are more likely to see and use the simpler, single, '6' and '9', with the double marks reserved for quotes within quotes:

> 'I've always loved the White Garden,' she said, adding, 'but while Vita always maintained that it gave her the "most exquisitely lasting pleasure on a moonlit evening", it was during the day that it charmed me most.'

One of the more contentious points of punctuation is where the full stop should go – inside or outside the quotation marks. As with parentheses, if the stop (or comma, question mark or exclamation mark) relates to the quoted material, it should go *inside* the quotation marks, otherwise outside. The above is correct, as is:

> She remembered hearing Vita saying that it 'always gave her most pleasure on moonlit evenings'.

She asked, 'Did Vita say that the garden gave her most pleasure on moonlit evenings?'

Note that the quotation in the first example is not a complete sentence; the second example is.

You will have noted from your reading of newspapers and books that quotation marks are used for several other purposes, including idiomatic expressions (*He said the best thing for him would be to 'take a powder'*).

The Errant Apostrophe

Catastrophes with apostrophes are everyday occurrences. A flower stall offers *Lilie's, Anemone's* and *Mum's; bargain T-shirt's* and *shell suit's* are advertised in the local freesheet. A notice at a school announced: *This School and it's Playground will be Closed over Easter.* The confusion isn't helped, either, when a wordsmith of the stature of Tennyson leaves us with these immortal lines:

> Their's not to make reply,
> Their's not to reason why,
> Their's but to do and die: . . .

Their's? Their is? Their's is? Nobody has ever quite worked out what was on Tennyson's mind, but he certainly left us with a cute conundrum.

Actually, handling apostrophes is really a straightforward matter. But first, you must recognise that there are two kinds of apostrophes: one to indicate a contraction – that is, a word with some letters left out – and one to indicate possession of something:

> My God! Did you hear? London's burning!
> I hope London's fire services can cope!

In the first statement, the apostrophe is used to shorten the word *is* in *London is burning*; in the second, the apostrophe tells us that the fire services belong to London. Here are some simple examples:

POSSESSIVE APOSTROPHES	CONTRACTION APOSTROPHES
Michael's mountain bike	*She'll be here soon* (she will)
the girl's tunic	*It is six o'clock* (of the clock)
the girls' gym	*I won't do it* (will not)
St James's Square	*It's not fair* (it is)

So far, so good, but let's look a little closer at each kind of apostrophe in turn.

Possessive Apostrophes

To show that a noun possesses, has or belongs to something, an *-s* is usually added. In the case of singular nouns:

> *a dog's collar*; *a man's suit*; *that woman's dress*;
> *Beryl's garden*; *the country's problems*; *a day's work*

The same rule applies to plural nouns that don't end with an *-s*:

> *women's preferences*; *children's books*; *mice's tails*

Where common nouns, whether singular or plural, end with *-s*, we simply add an apostrophe after the *-s*. But with proper nouns we have the choice of adding *-'s* or an apostrophe without the extra *-s*, according to tradition or how it sounds. You won't see *girls's* as the plural form of *girl's*, but you will see *Charles's* and *Charles'*. Some more examples:

> *The Jones's house, Jesus' teachings, measles' after-effects, Glynis's career, teachers' meetings, Wales' ruggedness*

Sometimes the choice is arbitrary; you will probably see *Jesus's teachings* as often as the alternative.

94

Despite Tennyson, pronouns do not normally require apostrophes (an exception is one's):

> *its shadow, the car is theirs, the victory is ours*

If you own a name you are entitled to do what you want with it, and many institutions and businesses are exercising this option and dropping apostrophes: *Missing Persons Bureau, Lloyds Bank, Gas Consumers Council, Womens Institute, Pears Soap.* And don't be caught out with James Joyce's *Finnegans Wake*, Thornton Wilder's *The Ides of March* and E. M. Forster's *Howards End*; they are titles, and none has apostrophes.

Contraction Apostrophes

The use of apostrophes for informal contractions is relatively straightforward:

hasn't	= has not	*I'm*	= I am
can't	= cannot	*it's*	= it is
there's	= there is	*let's*	= let us
mustn't	= must not	*I've*	= I have

Apostrophes are also used to concertina combinations like *shake'n'bake, sweet'n'low*; to drop the final letters of words like *finger lickin'* and *nuthin' doin'*; and to pluralise numbers and abbreviations: *1890's, MP's, CV's*, etc., although these are increasingly showing up without apostrophes: *1890s, MPs, CVs*.

But from all this, all you really need to remember is:

- *it's* is short for *it is*, and *its* indicates possession
- *who's* is short for *who is*; *whose* indicates possession

Twenty Sore Points

English grammar isn't like concrete which, once it hardens, never shifts. On the contrary, the language and its usage are always on the move. Arguments about its use erupt every day: in newspaper and publishing offices, in the law courts, in schools, at teachers' conferences, on trains, in pubs. You begin to wonder if the language and the rules that govern it were invented yesterday instead of several centuries ago.

The truth is that none of us always speaks and writes perfect, copper-bottomed English. Each of us has blind spots, rules we can never remember, concepts we never seem to understand, words of different meaning that sound the same or are spelt the same and which invariably confuse us.

Here are twenty 'sore points' of usage. There could be fifty, or fifteen hundred: the list could go on. But these have been selected for discussion because they seem to crop up so regularly.

-ISE OR -IZE   Although the *-ize* ending (derived from the Greek) is used in the US, in Britain there is a distinct preference for *-ise*. In this book, for example, *-ise* and *-isation* are used throughout. Many words, though, have always been spelt *-ise*: *advise*, *enterprise*, *despise*, *surprise*, etc. A few can look odd with the *-ise* ending (*capsise*) so are best left with *-ize*.

HOPEFULLY   The furore over the adverb *hopefully*, as used in sentences like

> Hopefully, the weather will improve this afternoon.

is based on a misunderstanding. In fact, the word, meaning *it is hoped*, has a perfectly legitimate parentage, albeit German. It began life as *hoffentlich*, meaning *I hope so*, and travelled with German immigrants to the US last century. During its stay there it was translated as *hopefully*, and now, as we all know, it is one of America's major exports to Britain, selling alongside the original adverb *hopefully*, meaning *full of hope*.

LAY AND LIE   The confusion between these verbs arises from the tenses:

| lay | laid | laid |
| lie | lay | lain |

The confusion is removed if you can remember that *to lay* is to put or set down something, while *to lie* is to recline. You *lay down the law, an egg is laid; you lie on the floor, she lay there and cried, she had lain there all night.*

DOUBLE NEGATIVES   Listen to this imaginary conversation:

> 'I didn't do nuffink, officer!'
> 'Well, if you didn't do nothing, you must have done something, right?'
> 'I didn't never do nuffink, honest!'
> 'That's all right, then. On your way!'

Here we have a double negative in the first line, which logically reverses the meaning, so the policeman is correct. But he is also correct – logically – in the last line, for he recognises that his would-be culprit has used three negatives, thus turning the double negative back to positive.

Why we should pick on this so-called uneducated usage is a mystery when educated French accepts and even requires it (*Je ne regrette rien: I don't regret nothing*) and educated English perpetrates double negatives (under the polite term of litotes) like *I'm not unhappy with the result*. But, in general, avoid.

WHILE AND WHILST   The latter is legitimate and means the same as *while*, but why use the longer word?

THAT, WHICH AND WHO   *That* can refer to persons, animals and things; *which* to animals and things; *who* and *whom* to persons only. There was a rule to use *that* to define the meaning or intention of the preceding word or phrase: *The car that Bruce drove down here has packed up*. *That* defines or identifies the car for us: the one he drove down here. The rule advised using *which* when the identifying information is already supplied in the sentence: *The old supercharged Bentley which Bruce drove down here has packed up*.

With persons, *that* is used to refer to any person, and *who* to a particular person: *The bloke that bought Bruce's Bentley lives in Birmingham. My cousin, who bought Bruce's Bentley, has money to burn*.

SPELLED AND SPELT   There are a number of verbs in this category:

> spell, dwell, smell, spill, spoil, kneel,
> lean, learn, leap, burn, dream

Although there is a strong and growing preference for -*t* endings, your options are still open. The -*ed* endings are almost universal in the US.

METAPHORICAL MIXTURES   *The manager of the football club admitted that he had several irons in the fire but he was keeping them close to his chest*. British Rail said that it has *a number of crossings in the pipeline, but these will now be put on ice*. A company chairman said that *they had stood on the edge of a precipice for too long and it was now time for a major step forward.* A Radio 3 announcer: *The artist has given full reign to his marvellous ear for colour.*

These are mixed metaphors, and eternal vigilance is the price you must pay to avoid them. Always remember the famous utterance of British Leyland's Sir Alfred Sherman: *So long as there is a crock of gold at the end of the garden the spur to sink or swim is blunted.* Or read *Jeremiah, iv, 4 (Authorised Version).*

LESS AND FEWER Use *fewer* for numbers and plural nouns; *less* for size and non-count nouns: *At the festival, fewer pints were drunk and less beer was consumed.*

ONLY This is a subversive word which, depending upon where it is placed in a sentence, can change its entire meaning. When we use *only* conversationally we use stresses to make our meaning clear; unfortunately we cannot do this when we use it in writing. For example:

A I can only lend you £10.
B I can lend you only £10.

Each of these two sentences means something different. A actually means I can't give you £10 but I can lend you that amount; while B means I can lend you £10 but that's the limit – I can't lend you any more.

Using *only* unambiguously requires care. The same goes for words like *merely, even, mainly, also* and *just:*

I just saw the film, not the play.
I saw just the film, not the play.

CAN AND MAY *Can* relates to possibility, while *may* relates to permission. This was once taught with a scrap of dialogue which went something like this:

PUPIL:	Please, Teacher, can I go to the toilet?
TEACHER:	Yes, John, you can, because you know where it is and you have two legs and so you are perfectly able to go to the toilet. The question is, will I allow you to go?
PUPIL:	Oh, please, Teacher, may I go to the toilet?

The same shadings, of course, apply to *could* and *might*, but such distinctions have now become hopelessly blurred in everyday usage.

QUITE   This is a word to use carefully as it has two meanings:

> I'm quite certain that Paloma will win the Derby.
> He's great at swimming and quite good with the bat.

You can see why *quite* can play tricks. In the first example it qualifies and strengthens *certain* so that it means something like, *I'm absolutely certain* . . . But in the second example it weakens the word it qualifies, the resulting meaning being, *Well, he's good with the bat, but not that good* . . .

SPLIT INFINITIVES   Gallons of metaphorical blood have been spilt over this legendary grammatical no-no, rather pointlessly as it turns out. The situation today is that the careful user has nothing against the occasional split infinitive, but would prefer to do the splitting consciously rather than unconsciously.

Curiously, it is impossible to split an infinitive, which is the grammatical term for a basic verb like *grow* (from which spring *growing*, *grew* and *grown*). The so-called split infinitive results from an adverb or adverbial phrase being placed between to and the infinitive: *He wanted his son to confidently grow into the job he'd created for him*. A purist would either write *He wanted his son confidently to grow into the job he'd created for him*, or rephrase the sentence.

The trouble with many unsplit infinitives is that they can be grossly inelegant and very much out of whack with everyday speech. They can also sometimes result in ambiguity: *The Government is attempting dramatically to increase the number of people in higher education*. What is meant, presumably, is that the proposed increase will be dramatic, but here it looks as though it is the attempt itself that is full of drama. A split infinitive – *to dramatically increase* – in this case conveys the required meaning with precision.

If Elizabeth Taylor's intention is *to never drink again* or *never to drink again*, few people are going to split hairs over it. Glasnost has been declared on the split infinitive, but it is still way short of total freedom.

THAT   In the interests of economy it is acceptable to drop *that* from sentences providing the meaning remains clear:

> She sincerely believed that she was in love with him.
> She sincerely believed she was in love with him.

WHO AND WHOM   Many grammar books devote several pages to this perplexing pair, but for practical purposes a simple rule exists to keep you out of trouble. If you relate *he* to *who*, and *him* to *whom*, you are halfway there (it doesn't quite work with *she/who* and *her/whom*). When in doubt, simply substitute *he* or *him*:

> I couldn't find out who/whom had the tickets.

In this case, you wouldn't say *him might have the tickets*, but *he* (or, indeed, *she*) *might have the tickets*. Therefore *who* would be correct. Or:

Who/whom are you slagging off to your friends?

Here, we might ask, am I slagging *he* off? No, it must be, am I slagging *him* off?, so *whom* would be correct. It would also be pompous and pedantic to announce '*Whom are you slagging off to your friends?*', which is why, increasingly, people are confining themselves to safer *who* territory.

DIFFERENT TO, FROM, OR THAN The first two are acceptable, with a general preference for *from*. *Different than* is common usage in the US.

IF AND WHETHER *If* is a versatile word but its use to replace *whether* can lead to ambiguity:

Did you notice if he had dandruff?

places the emphasis on *noticing*; if the observer wasn't alert he or she wouldn't notice whether he even had hair. The question that should have been asked to get the required answer is:

Did you notice whether or not he had dandruff?

WHATEVER This word has been hijacked from its correct meaning, which is *no matter what*: *Whatever the difficulties, we will succeed.* Nowadays we are more likely to hear: *He's a real DIY nut, you know, laying tiles, plastering, painting, fixing windows, whatever . . .* It looks and sounds sloppy, and it is.

EACH AND EVERY Most of us know that *each* requires a singular verb because it concerns a single person. But so does *every*; when you talk about every person in the room you are really referring to each and every single one:

Each man, woman and child in there has some complaint.
Every man, woman and child in there has some complaint.

However, when *each* is preceded by a plural subject it needs a plural verb:

Their uniforms were each given a thorough going-over by the drill sergeant.

YOU AND I AND YOU AND ME   A rule that usually works for most people is to think of *you* and *I* as *we*, and *you* and *me* as *us*.

We are a terrific couple – *You and I* are a terrific couple.
They're calling *us* liars – They're calling *you and me* liars.

To test such statements:

You and me are going to be late – *Us* is going to be late.
You and I are going to be late – *We* are going to be late.

The second statement passes the test, and is correct.

Grammatical Gamesmanship

Here's a little reward for doing all that hard work: some amusing grammatical games and puzzles.
Answers on page 107.

A Pile of Pairs

Parts of the human body excepted, how many items can you list that are usually referred to as a pair, such as trousers, shoes and gloves? Try for twenty.

That's That!

This is considered to be the ultimate punctuation test. Try punctuating *That that is is that that is not is not but that that is not is not that that is nor is that that is that that is not.*

Be Your Own Subeditor

This report appeared in the Boston *Herald American*:

> By then, Mrs Costello will have shed 80 of the 240 pounds she weighed in with when she entered the Peter Bent Brigham hospital obesity program. A third of her left behind!

How would you rewrite this? Discuss with friends.

Prepositional Pile-up

From time to time readers of newspapers are challenged to invent a sentence ending in as many prepositions as possible. A string of five comes with this chestnut: 'The little girl complained to her mother about her bedtime storybook: "What did you bring that book that I didn't want to be read *to out of up for?*" This, in turn, was stretched to nine prepositions in Godfrey Snith's column in *The Sunday Times*: 'What did you want to bring that book, that I didn't want to be read *to from out of, about Down Under, up for?*'

This effort is, however, still well short of the world record, offered by an American woman living in Illinois: 'What did you turn your socks from *inside in to inside out instead of from outside out to inside in for?*' That's fourteen. Can you do better?

Punctuation Playtime

What are some well-known words that contain:
1. A hyphen and an apostrophe?
2. Two hyphens and an apostrophe?
3. Three hyphens and an apostrophe?
4. No hyphens but two apostrophes?

Selling Books to Old Children

Here's a book dealer's ad. Is he selling children's books that are old or books that appeal to older children? How would you rewrite it to make this clear?

OLD CHILDREN'S BOOKS/ANNUALS

Closing down sale, thousands to clear. List requirements with SAE please to: John, 88 Watford Road, Birmingham B30 1PD

Poetic Punctuation

Can you repunctuate this rhyme so that it makes sense?

Every lady in the land
  Has twenty nails upon each hand,
Five and twenty on hands and feet.
  This is true, and no great feat.

Answers to Grammatical Games

A PILE OF PAIRS   Boots, cufflinks, leotards, mittens, pants, plimsolls, shorts, slacks, slippers, socks, stockings, suspenders, underpants, binoculars, eyeglasses, spectacles, bookends, chopsticks, earrings, pliers, skis, scissors, tweezers, tongs. Plus all the others you've thought of.

THAT'S THAT   Follow this closely: *That that is, is; that that is not, is not; but that that is not is not that that is; nor is that that is that that is not.* No? Try again.

PUNCTUATION PLAYTIME   Here are some of the words asked for, and there are doubtless others:

1. *bull's-eye   cat's-eye* (wildflower)   *cat's-tail* (species of reed)
2. *jack-o'-lantern*
3. *will-o'-the-wisp   cat-o'-nine-tails*
4. *fo'c'sle* (forecastle of a ship)

POETIC PUNCTUATION   With this punctuation, the poem makes sense:

Every lady in the land
   Has twenty nails. Upon each hand
Five, and twenty on hands and feet.
   This is true, and no great feat.

Read on

If *Good Grammar in One Hour*

- has broken the grammatical ice for you;
- has made you aware of what you and others are doing when speaking, writing and reading;
- has helped you to correct and avoid grammatical mistakes;

and, especially,

- has interested and intrigued you to the extent that you wish to know more about using the English language,

then *One Hour Wordpower* can ask for no more. But this little book is only what its cover says it is: a quick trip through the timeless territory of language. It's a territory that's well worth exploring, and any of the books listed here will prove to be valuable and user-friendly guides. Most are available in cheaper paperback format.

Bryson, Bill. *Mother Tongue – The English Language*. London: Penguin Books, 1990

Cobuild (COLLINS Birmingham University International Language Database). *English Grammar*. London and Glasgow: Collins Publishers, 1990

Cobuild. *Student's Grammar*. London: Harper Collins, 1991

Crystal, David. *Rediscover Grammar*. London: Longmans, 1992

Crystal, David. *Who Cares About English Usage?* London: Penguin Books, 1984

Crystal, David (ed). *Eric Partridge in His Own Words*. London: André Deutsch, 1980

Fowler, H. W. *A Dictionary of Modern English Usage*.

(Revised by Sir Ernest Gowers). Oxford: Oxford
University Press, 1965–1991

Gowers, Sir Ernest. *The Complete Plain Words*.
London: Guild Publishing, 1986

Greenbaum, Sidney. *An Introduction to English
Grammar*. London: Longman, 1991

Greenbaum, S. and Whitcut, Janet. *Guide to English
Usage*. London: Longman, 1988

Howard, Philip. *The State of the Language*. London:
Penguin Books, 1984

Leech, Geoffrey. *An A-Z of English Grammar & Usage*.
London: Nelson, 1989

Partridge, Eric. *Usage and Abusage*. London: Penguin
Books, 1990

Partridge, Eric. *You Have a Point There*. London:
Routledge, 1983

Roberts, Philip Davies. *Plain English: A User's Guide*.
London: Penguin Books, 1987

Thomson, A. J. and Martinet, A. V. *A Practical English
Grammar*. Oxford: Oxford University Press, 1986

Times, The. English Style and Usage Guide. London:
Times Books, 1992

Todd, Loreto, and Hancock, Ian. *International English
Usage*. London: Routledge, 1990

Waldhorn, Arthur, and Zeiger, Arthur. *English Made
Simple*. London: Made Simple Books (Butterworth-
Heinemann), 1991

Waterhouse, Keith. *English Our English (and how to
sing it)*. London: Viking, 1991

In addition to the above, companion volumes to *Good
Grammar in One Hour* in the *One Hour Wordpower*
series will help you to understand and appreciate
other aspects of the language in the same relaxed,
no-nonsense style.

These are widely available now:

Word Bank. Over 500 selected words to add colour and elegance to your speech and writing.

Word Check: Are You Using Words Correctly? Over 500 words most frequently used incorrectly.

Guide to Wordplay and Word Games. From acrostics and alternades, clerihews and spoonerisms, to word chains and word squares.

The Name Book. A fascinating book about surnames, given names, nicknames, changed names and eponyms. With spelling and pronunciation guide.

The Secrets of Speed Reading. A progressive do-it-yourself course of rapid reading with enhanced comprehension.

Crisp, Clear Writing in One Hour. Out with jargon, gobbledegook and lame, dull English; in with clear, crisp writing that commands attention and respect.

Spell Check. One thousand of the world's most misspelled words.